EARTHEN VESSELS

 *This book is published in cooperation with the* Association of Theological Schools in the United States and Canada

EARTHEN VESSELS

Hopeful Reflections
on the Work and Future
of Theological Schools

Daniel O. Aleshire

WILLIAM B. EERDMANS PUBLISHING COMPANY
GRAND RAPIDS, MICHIGAN / CAMBRIDGE, U.K.

Published 2008 by
Wm. B. Eerdmans Publishing Co.
2140 Oak Industrial Drive N.E., Grand Rapids, Michigan 49505 /
P.O. Box 163, Cambridge CB3 9PU U.K.

Printed in the United States of America

14 13 12 11 10 09 08   7 6 5 4 3 2 1

Library of Congress Cataloging-in-Publication Data

Aleshire, Daniel O., 1947-
Earthen vessels: hopeful reflections on the work and
future of theological schools / Daniel Aleshire.
p.   cm.
Includes bibliographical references.
ISBN 978-0-8028-6361-4 (pbk.: alk. paper)
1. Theological seminaries — United States.
2. Theology — Study and teaching — United States.
3. Theological seminaries — Canada.
4. Theology — Study and teaching — Canada.
I. Title.

BV4030.A74   2008
230.071'173 — dc22
                              2008010807

www.eerdmans.com

For Jo

Res severa est verum gaudium

Contents

Acknowledgments

I know very little that I have not been taught. I have been taught in schools and in conversations with thoughtful people, as well as by opportunities to work with and speak to theological schools. I have learned so much from others, over so many years, that the lines blur between what I have learned from others and what I have thought for myself. I am indebted to all these teachers and teaching moments, and, while unnamed, they must be acknowledged.

I am indebted to many others who should be thanked by name. The 2006-2008 officers of The Association of Theological Schools — Donald Senior, Cynthia Campbell, John Kinney, Leland Eliason, and Thomas Johnson — supported this work both by their having been granted release from administrative responsibilities during summer 2007 and by their thoughtful responses to drafts of the manuscript. Former presidents of the Association David Tiede, Martha Horne, and Robert Cooley read parts or all of the manuscript and provided insightful counsel. All of these people are cogent thinkers and effective institutional leaders. They care deeply about theological education and have been wonderful teachers and conversation partners.

Charles Foster and Charles Wood have devoted some of their varied scholarly attention to the study of theological education. They have taught me by their writing and by their reflections on an earlier draft of this manuscript. Barbara Wheeler has been a wise and incisive colleague for twenty-five years and has done as much as anyone in North America to discern and communicate issues related to theological education. Richard Mouw knows as much as any person I know, and I get to work with people who know a great deal. He is as generous with his knowledge as he is knowledgeable. G. Douglass Lewis and Faith Rohrbough have both retired from successful seminary presidencies and worked adjunctively with ATS for the past several years. Their institutional wisdom makes them wonderful teachers to people like me. I am grateful to all of these persons for their helpful reactions to this manuscript.

Michael Gilligan, who was an ATS staff colleague before moving to the Henry Luce Foundation, where he now serves as president, understands theological schools intimately well and is invariably wise and helpful. His comments were especially instructive. Two current colleagues on the ATS staff, Nancy Merrill, Director of Communications, and Carol Lytch, Assistant Executive Director, read the text with care and provided editorial improvements and helpful critiques. I also want to thank Linda Trostle, who verified references and provided editorial support, and Kathy Furlong, for her editorial help.

Craig Dykstra and John Wimmer, both of Lilly Endowment Inc., contribute to religion in North America, including theological education, by their wisdom, commitment, and knowledge. This manuscript was completed as part of a grant made to The Association of Theological Schools by Lilly Endowment.

Jon Pott, Vice President and Editor in Chief at Wm. B. Eerdmans Publishing, and his colleagues contributed support as well as the editorial and publishing skills necessary to make this book possible. The Association of Theological Schools is grateful for the partnership it has with the Eerdmans Publishing Company.

And finally, a personal word for Jo, who has given not only the time and space necessary to write this manuscript, but also the support and partnership that has made my work with theological schools possible. She is a person of intelligence, grace, and tenacity, with many interests and even more talents.

DA

Introduction

It was an emotional moment. So emotional, in fact, that remembering it brings the feelings back. It was my first year as an assistant professor, and I was preparing to preach a seminary chapel service for the first time. This seminary had a large enrollment and a chapel that could hold most of it. It was an imposing space; its architecture invited only important things to be said. As I prepared that sermon, my anxiety grew as I thought about three pews toward the front, on the left side, where faculty usually sat. Most of the people attending the service would be students, but the faculty were ever present in my thoughts while I was preparing. Preaching to the students was energizing; preaching to my colleagues, all of whom that year were my *senior* colleagues, was intimidating.

I scoured texts and thought about subjects, but finally decided on the one thing that I had studied most in the preceding years: the nature of ministry. The text was from 2 Corinthians, in which Paul defends his ministry from attack and, in the context, develops a theological statement about Christian ministry as a whole. "But we have this treasure [the work of ministry] in earthen vessels . . ." he wrote. From that sermon forward, the image of "earthen vessels" has been part of my association with theological schools. I taught a required course each year for entering students called "Formation for Ministry." The first two weeks of most of these courses were spent reading and reflecting with students on the extended text in 2 Corinthians. "We have this treasure in clay jars . . ." (NRSV). A jar has value only to the extent that it fulfills its function. Ministry is like that — and this is Paul's point. Ministry is never about the minister; it is always about the gospel the minister proclaims.

Like ministry, theological schools are earthen vessels. Earthen vessels are remarkably durable. Archeological excavations of ancient sites often unearth pottery shards, and occasionally, intact vessels. These vessels could still hold water, thousands of years after they were formed. There are not many things millennia old that can still be used. The long useful life of earthen vessels can also be the case for theological schools. While durable, earthen vessels are also fragile. If dropped, they break. Careless use can damage them. The same is true for theological schools. They require care and attention in order to last. The earthen vessels of the biblical text were formed by hand. They had irregularities and imperfections and lacked the uniformity of mass-produced pottery ware. Theological schools are, once again, like earthen vessels. They differ from each other in significant ways, yet they serve a similar purpose. Imperfections of many sorts abound, but the schools still function. Earthen vessels, unlike wineskins, can hold both new wine and old wine. At a time when change is a dominant characteristic of religious life in North America, it is reassuring that a resource, like a vessel, that served in one way in an earlier time can serve in another way in another time. Likening theological schools to mud that has been shaped and baked has its limitations, but it is an image that has resonated with me as long as I have been working in theological education. I want to make the case, once again, for the importance of these earthen vessels.

Descriptive and Appreciative Reflections

Much of the literature on theological education tends to be either historical or analytic. The historical literature is valuable because theological schools provide an important lens on the growth and, sometimes, decline of religious communities. Institutional histories, at least the best of them, define larger religious contexts and tell the stories of leaders who fashioned new religious movements or renewed established ones. The analytic literature tends to situate current educational practices in the context of historic aims and purposes of theological education. On the basis of its analysis, this literature argues for changes that will make it better. The intent of this project is neither historical, although it reflects the historical literature, nor analytic, although it depends heavily on this scholarly literature. The approach in this book is descriptive and reflects an evaluative strategy known as appreciative inquiry.

While much of the literature about theological education traces history, analyzes problems, and proposes changes, it tends not to describe the educational work and institutional practices of these schools. As a result, seminaries remain more mysterious than is good for them or for the constituents they serve. I want to describe what these schools do when they are working at their best, when they are doing what they were designed to do. The description is not about the demographics of these schools — their students, finances, enrollments, and facilities — but their fundamental processes — learning, teaching, research, governing, and administering.

Theological schools in North America are attracting a range of serious questions these days. Mainline Protestant denominations are credentialing an increasing number of clergy without post-baccalaureate theological education because many of their congregations can no longer support full-time pastors. Evangelical megachurches have argued that theological education should be centered in successful congregations rather than theological schools, and there is some evidence that larger Evangelical congregations discount the education provided by theological schools. Roman Catholics are experiencing an unprecedented growth in the number of lay professional parish staff who are responsible for many aspects of parish life and ministry. Parishes and episcopal leaders, however, are unsure of the amount of theological education these persons need to do their work well. These changes in the perceptions and practices of parishes and congregations result in questions about the value of theological schools. Is there a continuing role for their historic missions as this new century develops? Should the pattern of theological education that has served North American Christianity well in the past be jettisoned in the future?

In light of these fundamental questions, I want to take an appreciative look at the work of theological schools. There are two ways to examine this type of organization or social system. The first is to identify problems and make proposals about how to solve them. This is by far the dominant strategy in analyses of theological schools. The second, less common, method is to identify strengths that are evident when an organization is functioning at its best and make proposals about how these strengths can best support future work. Sue Hammond describes the traditional approach this way: "The primary focus is on what is wrong or broken; since we look for problems, we find them. By paying attention to problems, we emphasize and amplify them." She then notes that appreciative inquiry "suggests that we look for what works in an organization. The tangible result of the inquiry process . . . describe[s] where the organization wants to be, based on the high moments of where [it has] been."[1] Theological schools have considerable educational vitality and institutional durability, more than problem-focused literature would suggest. Appreciative inquiry strategists would contend that these strengths are the qualities most crucial for understanding theological schools and their potential contribution in the future.

Appreciative inquiry does not focus on idealized strengths or hoped-for abilities that have never existed in the organization, but on real, demonstrated strengths. While it does not ignore problems and concerns, it does not presume that fixing current problems is the most effective way of strengthening an organization for the future. This essay seeks to explore theological schools in terms of what they were invented to do, what they have learned to do well, and the significant contribution that they can make in the future.

1. Sue Annis Hammond, *The Thin Book of Appreciative Inquiry,* 2nd ed. (Bend, Ore.: Thin Book Publishing Company, 1998), pp. 6-7.

Sources and Audience

For almost two decades, I have had the privilege of working with the theological schools that are members of The Association of Theological Schools in the United States and Canada (ATS).[2] Through the educational and applied research of the Association and the accreditation activities of its Commission on Accrediting, my work at ATS provides a privileged access to these schools — from their serious self-examination in preparation for accrediting reviews, to thoughtful conversations at conferences, to consultations with seminary leaders — and this access has granted insight into the hopes and fears of these schools, their capacities and frailties, their successes and failures. ATS schools include the broad range of North American Christianity — mainline Protestant, Evangelical Protestant, Roman Catholic, and Orthodox — and very few settings in North America provide the privilege of working across this wide spectrum. Much of what I know about theological schools has come from what the schools have taught me during my tenure at ATS.

The ATS standards of accrediting are mentioned often in this essay. The current standards were adopted after four years of work to redevelop previous standards from a zero base. Because the standards are adopted by vote of the member schools, they constitute a formal expression of the understandings and practices to which the schools have agreed to be held accountable. The standards both describe mini-

2. The Association of Theological Schools in the United States and Canada was founded in 1918 and includes in its membership more than two hundred fifty schools in North America. The Association's primary functions include collecting data on a wide range of issues in theological education and providing resources that make those data useful to the schools and the broader public; producing publications and other forms of communication with member schools and, on their behalf, for the broader public; developing projects to address issues in theological education or to help schools acquire needed skills for their work; and conducting a range of programs for the professional development of administrative leaders and faculty. The Commission on Accrediting of the Association of Theological Schools is a separate but related corporation that conducts all of the activities related to the accreditation of schools that are members of the Association.

mal accrediting expectations and identify characteristics to which schools should aspire. As such, they have the unique status of describing what the schools think they should be, when they are functioning at their best.

Another frequently cited resource is the research of the Auburn Center for the Study of Theological Education at Auburn Theological Seminary. Theological schools tend to rely on opinion and anecdote to describe their work. In the early 1990s, the Auburn Center was founded as a research center focused on theological education. It has conducted numerous studies across the past fifteen years, including projects about faculty in ATS schools, student characteristics, graduates' perceptions about their theological school experience, the attitudes and perceptions of members of governing boards, student debt, and a number of other issues. The results of this research provide some of the most useful information available about a range of issues in theological schools.

During the past decade, I have spoken to seminary trustees, seminary administrators, seminary faculty, and at times, denominational and pastoral leaders about theological education. Some speeches identified issues that needed more thought, and I have elected to pursue many of these thoughts in a more systematic way in this project. Since I have primarily addressed issues in theological schools over the past decade in speeches, I have chosen to write in a similar style, personally and conversationally. While I hope this essay is thoughtful, it should not be understood as a scholarly assessment. It is personal. It reflects my perceptions about the work of theological schools, not their perceptions of their own work or the perceptions of the scholars who have studied theological education most extensively.

It is also an essay written at a particular point in time. The end of the first decade of a new century is upon us. The Y2K worries of 1999 are all but forgotten. The computers worked, the lights stayed on, the cars started, and planes did not fall from the sky. The old century passed and a new one began, and much continued as it was. The forces and social trends that influenced North American Christianity for the last decades of the twentieth century have continued their influence in this one, and some new forces are emerging. The changes in religious practices and social presence of religion that became dominant at the end of the last century continue in this one, and more changes are becoming evident. Likewise, theological schools are dynamic organizations, as are the ecclesial communities to which they relate. They change with the times, and any analysis reflects the issues and concerns of the time during which the analysis was made. Fortunately, institutions do not change so fast that what is true one day is not true the next.

Because I am writing conversationally, I want you to know the groups with whom I most want to have the conversation: the people that make these schools work. They include board members, donors, administrators, and faculty.

The persons who serve on governing boards are an invaluable resource for theological schools. While seminaries maintain meaningful relationships with the denominations they serve, many have ceased to be the integrated units of their denominations that they once were. In those earlier times, boards tended to exercise an oversight role, but that is changing. Increasingly, theological schools depend on board members who understand the work of the school and who exercise leadership in their governance. At one time, clergy comprised the majority of board members. While this is still true for many schools, an increasing number of boards have a majority of lay persons who have never been to seminary. This essay is intended to inform board members about the broader community of theological schools and the ways in which the individual schools they serve are similar to or different from others.

In an earlier era, much of the funding for theological schools came from supporting denominations or ecclesial bodies. That has changed steadily and rapidly across the past forty years. Contributions from individuals comprise a large and growing percentage of the revenue necessary for these schools to attain their missions. Most donors do not give major gifts to these schools in pursuit of personal gratification. Gifts to other organizations will bring more status or community recognition. Rather, people give to theological schools because they care about the church and want to contribute to the quality of leadership it will have in the future. They care about the Christian faith and want to support the kind of scholarship that will refine its voice and strengthen its intellectual underpinnings. I am writing to donors in hopes that they will learn more about what theological schools do and why they are worth the treasure it takes to make them work.

Administrators come to theological schools from many kinds of previous service. Over the past five years, about half of the new presidents and deans have come from other roles in seminaries or higher education and the other half from pastorates or some form of denominational service. This is a very different pattern than in higher education, where most senior leaders were employed in higher education prior to their present position. Theological schools are small but complex institutions, and the guidance and ordering of that complexity invariably falls on administrators. I am writing as an administrative practitioner to other practitioners, in hopes that this essay can provide a frame of reference that enhances their understanding of the institutions they serve.

Faculty members work at the center of the theological school's educational mission, but in several discussions at ATS events, they have raised basic questions about the aims and purposes of theological schools. They are supportive of the work of the school, but have not always been able to distinguish between the educational mission and disciplinary specialization of *graduate* schools and the ministerial formation and disciplinary integration of *theological* schools. An excellent array of scholarly literature explores the aims and purposes of theological education; most of it was written by faculty in earlier decades,[3] which accounts for its high scholarly value. This literature is sufficiently expansive, however, that faculty are unlikely to study it in addition to the reading necessary for them to stay current in their fields. This essay is meant to provide faculty with a stimulus to their own corporate reflection as a new school year begins, or as they begin

---

3. David H. Kelsey and Barbara G. Wheeler, "Thinking about Theological Education: The Implications of 'Issues Research' for Criteria of Faculty Excellence," *Theological Education* 28, no. 1 (Autumn 1991).

work on an institutional self-study, or as individuals join a theological faculty for the first time.

Finally, I hope that church and denominational leaders might find this essay useful. This is an era in which financial pressures, the increasing need for locally available education for part-time and alternately credentialed clergy, and the increasing debt of seminary graduates invite questions about the value of the education provided by theological schools. These are important questions, ones that occupy schools as well as denominational leaders. In the midst of them, the schools have an important contribution to make to the future of the church and its ministry. I hope that this essay reminds church leaders of their own experience in seminary and generates ideas about the ways in which theological schools can be a resource in the many changes denominations and ecclesial bodies are experiencing.

Content

This book is organized in three parts: issues related to a case for theological schools, the tasks related to the work of the schools, and the partners with whom theological schools do their work.

Chapter 1 explores issues related to the case for theological schools. In law, a case statement is about the facts of the case and, potentially, issues related to legal process or precedent. Proposals for funding special projects often have case statements identifying the need and value of the project or task. I am not writing a case for the financial support of theological schools, even though they need financial support, deserve that support, and will not survive without it. This essay is a statement of the case for theological schools that I will make by describing the work they were invented to do and the valuable contributions they make when that work is done well.

Chapters 2 and 3 focus on the work of the schools, that is, theological scholarship — which includes the interrelated activities of teaching, learning, and research. While the term "scholarship" is often used as a synonym for "research," the ATS accrediting standards link teaching, research, and learning. ATS faculty members often comment on the relationship between teaching and research. While course preparation, teaching, and interaction with students are time-consuming, most faculty concur that students ask important questions, and that in other, less direct ways, their teaching and interaction with students enhance their research. If faculty members are teaching well, they are also learning. Recently, a faculty member at Indiana University retired for health reasons following thirty-three years of teaching. He feared that he would miss teaching, but commented, "[I]t turns out that what I love most about academe is not teaching but learning."[4] Teaching, learning, and research are intimately related, but they are not only the work of faculty. They comprise the primary work of students as well. Teaching is often the best way for students to learn a subject, and sometimes students learn more in a class session they teach than one led by a professor. Student research projects and papers are, most importantly, a way of learning. They may not lead to publication like their teachers' research, but when done well, student research opens doors to new issues and deepens understanding. The primary work of theological schools is teaching, learning, and research.

Chapter 4 is about making the schools work. Good teaching, learning, and research do not occur in a vacuum. They require administration and governance, which constitute more than the support functions necessary for theological scholarship. Teaching, learning, and research can be badly hampered by poor governance or administration and greatly enhanced by dependably effective governance and administration.

Chapter 5 addresses issues related to the theological school's principal partners — the church and the higher education community — and its principal hope, the future. Theological schools are hybrid institutions. They are intimately and irrevocably related both to the work of the church and to the patterns and practices of higher education. This is an era of unrest in both partners, and much of the agenda that

---

4. Murray Sperber, "Why I Stopped Teaching and Don't Miss It," *The Chronicle of Higher Education*, 22 June 2007. Quoted in *The Christian Century*, 24 July 2007.

is presently before schools is a function of their relationship to both higher education and communities of faith. Much of the future of the schools will be framed by changes in these partners and the ways that schools change in response. If the church changes, theological schools should change, and if higher education changes, theological schools will change. The case for theological schools will rest on their responses and adaptations to these changes. It is a hopeful future, and the responses to these changes will create a future of considerable opportunities for theological schools.

CHAPTER I

The Case for Theological Schools

I grew up in a succession of three neighborhood congregations. None of them was unique.

The first church I remember is the one that my parents began attending after my father returned from World War II. There couldn't have been more than ten families who were active in this congregation, and the church had a succession of part-time pastors. I remember only one: he was a used car salesman during the week and pastor on the weekends. It was an interesting bi-vocational combination. This church became embroiled in controversy, which in a church that size is usually a conflict between families masquerading as a theological dispute. My family was on the losing side, which explains the move to the second church.

The second congregation was nearer the home my parents built in 1954. This church was a little bigger: it had a choir and a full-time pastor. My family was very involved in this church, as we had been in the previous congregation. My dad was a deacon and taught the adult Sunday school class; my mother worked with the youth and helped in other ways; my brother was the part-time sexton for a while. Early one summer, events turned tragic for my family and, within a year, church turned sour for me. My father was killed in an accident. At first, the church was a source of support and care. But in time, when my mother

I

began to date the man who would become my stepfather, hushed talk began — comments about disrespecting my father's memory and whether and when widows should remarry. My mother was devastated, and as her teenaged son, I was offended. My mother needed support, not judgment. I decided to go to church elsewhere.

The third congregation was somewhat larger, related to a different denomination, and unlike the first two, was growing. The volunteers in this church seemed to know how to do things — from music to educational programming. The preaching was different, as well. The sermons were easier to understand and used scripture more engagingly — at least it seemed that way to my tenth-grade hearing. The pastor was no doubt more talented than those in the first two churches, but he was also a seminary graduate. I had always attended churches whose denominations did not require seminary education for ordination. For the first time, I was in a church whose pastor had gone to seminary.

These congregations are different, now. One has closed, another is in decline, and one is doing better than it ever has. However faulty my memories of these churches may be, they have led to two abiding commitments. The first is that congregations, even not-so-good ones, can be deeply formative environments. These congregations often failed, but somehow faith was nurtured in me and I sensed a call to ministry as I participated in them. Grace will do its work in human lives no matter how poorly congregations do theirs. The second is that seminary education is an important resource for congregational ministry. There was a qualitative difference in the pastoral ministry of the third congregation compared to the first two.

I talked with that pastor as I was seeking to discern my own call to ministry. He spoke appreciatively about his seminary experience, and eventually I enrolled in the seminary from which he graduated. More than any other educational institution I have attended, seminary changed me. Theological education is formative and, in many cases, transformative. It weaves two powerful human activities, believing and learning, into a common cloth. Seminary affected parts of me that other schools never touched. I did not realize how much it impacted me at the time, but the longer I work in ministry, the more I find myself going back to seminary experiences that defined reality, defined me, and defined Christian faithfulness.

I want to make a case for theological schools. It begins with the perception that seminary education makes a difference in the quality of pastoral ministry, and it continues with the ongoing realization that seminary education, even with its educational failures and institutional foibles, was the most powerful educational experience of my life. A case for an enterprise as diverse as theological schools in North America cannot be based on one person's experience, but it would be inauthentic, at least for me, to try making a general case if the particular, experiential, one were not personally true.

Making a Case for This Century

Since the founding of Harvard College more than a century before the Revolutionary War, the North American continent has had theological schools in one form or another. The Association of Theological Schools now counts more than 250 seminaries, divinity schools, and schools of theology in its membership, with a combined enrollment of more than 80,000 students, and combined revenue of almost two billion dollars. Why do we need to make a case for a set of institutions that is now as large and diverse as the United States and Canada have ever had?

Twenty years ago, biblical scholar Walter Brueggemann wrote, "The case for theological education cannot finally be made once and for all. It needs to be made again and again, because what theology and theological education are called to do varies in each social setting and cultural circumstance."[1] Theological education is a socially constructed enterprise, and when times and issues change, the case for theological education needs to be reconsidered, if not reconstructed.

1. Walter A. Brueggemann, "The Case for an Alternative Reading." Originally published in *Theological Education* 23, no. 2 (Spring 1987); reprinted in Walter Brueggemann, *Interpretation and Obedience: From Faithful Reading to Faithful Living* (Minneapolis: Fortress Press, 1991), p. 100.

The times are changing.

In the early 1970s, seven ATS member schools developed a case for their work to use in an effort to obtain grants from foundations. These schools were either university-related or conducted research doctoral degrees jointly with universities. Their case statement began by noting a crisis of values: "In American society the traditional patterns of spiritual and moral life have been challenged or have already been shattered. . . ."[2] Most of the rest of the case that these schools made related to their university relationships and their nondenominational approach to theological education. The reason these theological schools wanted foundation support was so that they could speak to the new national debate about values. "Though drastic changes in religion may be ahead, religion will almost inevitably play a part in any new patterning of values."[3] It is not clear if the changes in the subsequent decades have been drastic, but they certainly have been noticeable.

Values continue to be an important aspect of cultural discourse, but the values that are being emphasized seem to have changed. The focus on progressive social values in the 1960s and 1970s has given way to conservative social values in the 1980s and 1990s. I don't think that this was the change in values that those seven schools were anticipating in 1972. It is not clear what values will become dominant in the early years of this new century. Whatever they are, religion in North America will have something to say about them.

These decades have also brought many changes to religion. The dominant expression of Protestantism has shifted. Mainline, or more liberal Protestantism, was dominant in the 1970s; Evangelicalism, or more conservative Protestantism, is the dominant form in the first decade of the twenty-first century. The number of Roman Catholics in North America has increased greatly across these forty years, but the

2. *The Case Statement for the Support of Theological Education in the 1970s* (January 1972): 2. The seven schools participating in this case statement included Graduate Theological Union, Harvard Divinity School, Union Theological Seminary, University of Chicago Divinity School, University of Notre Dame Department of Theology, Vanderbilt Divinity School, and Yale Divinity School.

3. *Case Statement*, p. 2.

percentage of Catholics who attend mass on a weekly basis has declined. While Christianity remains the overwhelmingly dominant religious expression in North America, the number of adherents to other world religions is growing. Religion remains a strong and viable presence in North America, but beneath this presence, currents are shifting.

Higher education in North America has also changed since the 1970s. This period has been marked by considerable growth and expansion. Community college systems have been developed, public institutions have grown, and most private colleges and universities are stronger than they were in the 1970s. While a few institutions have closed, most are more robust than they were forty years ago. Community colleges, extension campuses, and distance learning programs make higher education available to most people in North America without leaving home. As both the U.S. and Canada continue to shift from manufacturing to service and information economies, the importance of an educated citizenry continues to grow.

Theological schools are hybrid institutions — with part of their identity in the church and part of their identity in higher education. This unique character has implications both for the education that students encounter and the opportunities and stresses that schools experience. About the time that a student thinks that seminary is a church, he is confronted with a discouraging grade and discovers that he is in a school. About the time that a seminary student is convinced that seminary is only a school, she is overpowered by some text or discussion or lecture that touches her soul, and she experiences in school what only church has done in her life previously. Because theological schools are hybrid institutions, they experience a double portion of the pressures that higher education and religion encounter. At this time, this means that theological schools experience both the shifting currents in North American religion and the increasing pressure on higher education to demonstrate what students have learned, as well as the extent to which the goals of degree programs have been attained.

The Christian faith has an interesting perspective on time. Jesus was born in the "fullness of time." The conditions may not have been ideal for the Savior of the world to have been born, but the God of

5

ages past and years to come saw fullness, and determined that it was the right time to demonstrate God's remarkable love. The Bible has one word for the kind of time that passes, like the hours of the day, and another term for the kind of time that marks special opportunity. The changes in religion and higher education may be merely the kind of changes that come and go with the passing of years. Or, they may mark a special time — a unique historical moment when the opportunities outweigh the threat. It is never clear, in the middle of the day, which kind of time it is. I have a hunch it is a special time, a fullness of time, a special opportunity for theological schools and for religion.

Walter Brueggemann was right. "The case for theological education . . . needs to be made again and again, because what theology and theological education are called to do varies in each social setting and cultural circumstance." Theological schools must articulate a sufficiently compelling reason to invite new generations of board members, contributors, students, and faculty to sustain and improve these schools and take them into the future that they are called to serve. The case needs to be made for this time, perhaps a unique moment pregnant with opportunity, and to do that, two questions need to be addressed. The first concerns the diversity of theological schools. Can a common case be made for such a variety of unique schools? The second is about current questions and critiques of theological education, of which there are many. Can a case be made in a time when so many different kinds of questions are being posed about theological schools? I want to address these two questions, and then proceed to making the case.

Particular Schools and Common Experiences

That early 1970s case statement I mentioned was based on common characteristics of the seven schools that developed it, and the perception that, as a group, they were different from other theological schools in significant ways. Can a case be made for theological schools as a whole, with all their differences? I think so.

6

Particular Stories

I don't know if the devil is in the details, but I know that God is in the particulars. Christianity in North America is housed in particular congregations and traditions that refract Christian believing into a wide variety of doctrinal emphases, patterns of worship, and practices of faith. And, accordingly, theological schools are very particular institutions. Theological education in North America is anything but generic. Schools are as different from one another as they are, together, from colleges and universities. They exist for many reasons; they have diverse histories; they have varying patterns of educational programs; they serve very different students and constituencies. As a result, there are as many cases for the value of theological schools as there are schools. However, the stories of individual schools share common plots and contribute to shared understandings of the value and contributions of theological education. Consider the stories of five very different schools.

St. Mary's Seminary in Baltimore was founded not long after the Diocese of Baltimore was established in 1789. The founding of the Baltimore diocese was presumed necessary because a new nation, the United States, needed its own church, just as European nations had their own national Catholic Churches. Its first bishop, John Carroll, wanted a college and seminary "to perpetuate a succession of labourers in this vineyard,"[4] but he was unsure if the diocese had enough students or money to support a seminary. The seminary was made possible because the Society of Saint Sulpice, a French order of priests, was willing to send priests, funds, and even some students to start the new seminary, which was founded in 1791 — one of the earliest freestanding seminaries in the United States. The seminary was founded to cultivate indigenous American leadership for the Catholic Church, and to accomplish this it depended on a French order, French priests, French monetary support, and, to some extent, French students. St. Mary's

---

4. Joseph M. White, *The Diocesan Seminary in the United States: A History from the 1780s to the Present* (Notre Dame, Ind.: University of Notre Dame Press, 1989), p. 29.

was founded as a diocesan seminary, which is a seminary under the direct control of a bishop, a pattern of theological education that developed in the sixteenth century in response to the Protestant Reformation. The priests of the Society of St. Sulpice still oversee St. Mary's Seminary more than two centuries later, and the seminary continues as the diocesan seminary of the Archdiocese of Baltimore.

The Civil War had just ended. Slavery had been abolished, but newly freed men and women entered an economically shattered world as freed men and women, and racial prejudice and local laws ensured the continuation of a separate world for African Americans in the South. The American Baptist Home Missionary Society wanted to address the educational needs of these African Americans and started the National Theological Institute. In 1865, two of its branches were in Washington, DC and Richmond, Virginia. The Washington school became known as Wayland Seminary, named for the former president of Brown University who had been a leading advocate in the antislavery movement. The Richmond branch became known as Richmond Seminary. Washington proved to be a more hospitable environment for a school for African Americans than Richmond, the former capital of the Confederate States. The Richmond school even had difficulty finding a place to conduct classes. Much of the city had been burned as the Confederate troops vacated the city, and what remained was economically devastated. The school was finally able to rent a site known as Lumpkin's jail, which slave dealer Robert Lumpkin had used as a holding pen and "breaking" center. The first classroom for the education of freed slaves for ministry had whipping posts still standing in the room.

Though funded and initially staffed by Northern white Baptists, African American Baptists accepted the school as their own. Eventually, Wayland Seminary and Richmond Seminary merged to form Virginia Union University in 1899. The schools, founded for the education of African American ministers, expanded their mission to include baccalaureate education for men and women. Samuel DeWitt Proctor graduated from Virginia Union in the early 1940s and later served as its president. He then worked in senior positions in the Peace Corps and the Office of

Economic Opportunity, and served as pastor of the Abyssinian Baptist Church. He was a premier twentieth-century black leader, mentor, preacher, educator, and tireless advocate for African American leadership. The School of Theology at Virginia Union is named for this grandson of a woman born in slavery.[5]

Late in the nineteenth century, the Methodist Episcopal Church, South was seeking to identify a pattern for educating its preachers, but it was divided. The denomination had grown dramatically through the nineteenth century, and that growth reflected the work of ministers who were not university-trained. Some Southern Methodists thought that theological education would ruin piety and doctrinal fidelity. Others were convinced that the rising educational level of many lay people, as the South was beginning to recover from the devastation of the war, required a higher level of education for clergy. Those who favored more theological education, however, disagreed over the institutional form it should take. Some worried that a freestanding seminary, like St. Mary's in Baltimore, would siphon scarce funds from other works of the denomination. Others felt that money invested in education should extend to laity as well as clergy, and they supported the founding of a university that would have a theological school. In 1872, representatives gathered to consider the issue and determined that they would found a "great university" "of the highest order."[6] The Methodists concluded that a university would need at least a million dollars before it could start, but after solicitation across the South, contributions totaled only thirty thousand dollars. Holland McTyeire, one of two bishops at the 1872 meeting, stayed with Cornelius Vanderbilt during a visit to New York, and as a result of conversations during his visit, McTyeire returned to Tennessee with a commitment from Vanderbilt for five hundred thousand dollars and, with an additional

5. Samuel DeWitt Proctor's *The Substance of Things Hoped For: A Memoir of African American Faith* (Valley Forge, Pa.: Judson Press, 1999) was published after Proctor's death in 1997. It was reviewed by Mark R. Wilson in *Baptist History and Heritage,* Summer-Fall 2001, and these biographical notes are taken from that review.

6. Dale A. Johnson, ed., *Vanderbilt Divinity School: Education, Contest, and Change* (Nashville, Tenn.: Vanderbilt University Press, 2001), p. 45.

five hundred thousand dollars that Vanderbilt contributed two years later, Vanderbilt University was founded.[7]

Vanderbilt began with a "Biblical Department" that sought "to furnish the church ministers who in addition to a sound Christian experience, humble piety, and consecration to God, are learned in scripture, sound in doctrine, refined but simple in manners; earnest, direct, and plain in the presentation of the truth, and ready for any field of service to which the church may assign them."[8] It was not long, however, before a dispute over governance arose, particularly the role of bishops in the governance of the university. After the court sided with the board of the university and rejected the claims of the bishops, the Methodists disowned the university in 1914. Eventually, the Biblical Department became the nondenominational School of Religion. Its mission was broadened, its faculty began to include non-Methodists, and it sought to educate not only ministers but also specialized religious workers. Vanderbilt became one of the early twentieth-century university-related divinity schools that provided support for the emerging ecumenical tendencies in American Protestantism[9] and a more professional approach to clerical education.

The Methodists were up to something else in Canada. An ecumenical spirit and a desire for a national church for "Christian" Canada led Methodists, Presbyterians, and Congregationalists to consider merging. As these complex talks advanced, Knox College, the Presbyterian theological college, dedicated a new facility in 1915 that was to become the seminary of the newly united church. A minority of Presbyterians, however, determined at the last minute not to enter the

---

7. After the conflict that led the Methodists to withdraw from their relationship to Vanderbilt in 1914, Methodists in the South went on to establish Emory University and Southern Methodist University, and to continue affiliation with Trinity College as it became Duke University. The divinity schools of these three universities are the only United Methodist schools in the South.

8. Johnson, *Vanderbilt Divinity School*, p. 47.

9. Johnson, *Vanderbilt Divinity School*, p. 63. See also Conrad Cherry, *Hurrying Toward Zion: Universities, Divinity Schools, and American Protestantism* (Bloomington: Indiana University Press, 1995).

1925 merger, and it was left to the courts to decide who would get the stately, gothic campus of Knox College. The court awarded it to the continuing Presbyterian Church of Canada, even though 70 percent of the Presbyterians joined the Methodists, Congregationalists, and the Union Churches of Western Canada to form the United Church of Canada. The newly united church needed a seminary, and Emmanuel College was formed in 1928 as the merger of Union College (which had just recently been founded by the board, faculty, and students who left Knox College following the court's decision) and the formerly Methodist faculty of theology at Victoria University. The new school was named Emmanuel College, "God is with us."[10]

As Protestantism developed in the early decades of the twentieth century, most of the denominations "attempted to tone down the offenses to modern sensibilities of a Bible filled with miracles and a gospel that proclaimed human salvation from eternal damnation only through Christ's atoning work on the cross." But true to their name, some Protestants protested. "Fundamentalism was the response of traditionalist evangelicals who declared war on these modernizing trends."[11] War it was, especially in the United States. Protestant denominations were fractured and, in the process, a new kind of seminary emerged: the nondenominational Protestant seminary. There had been nondenominational seminaries, like Union Theological Seminary in New York, but like Union, these schools had been founded as denominational seminaries and became "nondenominational" as a result of conflict. Fuller Theological Seminary was founded as a nondenominational seminary in 1947. Its constituency was the Protestant heirs of the fundamentalist struggles of the 1920s and 1930s.

Charles Fuller was a radio evangelist, and in the early 1940s, Fuller's programs on the Mutual Broadcasting Network had larger audiences than programs featuring Bob Hope or Charlie McCarthy.[12]

---

10. http://www.vicu.utoronto.ca/emmanuel/aboutus/mission.htm; http://www.united-church.ca/history/overview/brief/.

11. George M. Marsden, *Reforming Fundamentalism: Fuller Seminary and the New Evangelicalism* (Grand Rapids: William B. Eerdmans Publishing Co., 1987), p. 4.

12. Marsden, *Reforming Fundamentalism*, p. 14.

When it was time to think about leadership succession in the ministry he had created, Fuller, along with Harold Ockenga, determined that the movement needed a seminary with a faculty of first-class Evangelical scholars. Ockenga provided institutional and intellectual guidance and Fuller gave his ability to rally supporters and raise money. They met in Chicago in the spring of 1947 and determined that the school should open that fall. The first solicitations for students were on Fuller's "Old Fashioned Revival Hour" program and, remarkably, the seminary opened that fall with thirty-nine students.[13] Fuller began independently of any ecclesiastical authority, with a collection of strong individualists for a faculty, a vision for a new kind of intellectually rigorous Evangelical scholarship, and sufficient resources to fund the vision. Sixty years later, Fuller Seminary enrolls more students than any other theological school in North America.

These are five very particular stories. No one would confuse one of these theological schools with another. The case for theological education is not generic, it is particular. The reason that Sulpicians oversee the education of priesthood candidates at St. Mary's today is different from the reason that Emmanuel College educates men and women in the progressive theological tradition of the United Church of Canada, which is different from the reason that Fuller Seminary educates students from more than one hundred denominations in an Evangelical Protestant perspective, which is different from the theological education of African American ministers at Virginia Union, which is different from how Vanderbilt University Divinity School provides nondenominational theological education in a research university context. Each school has a particular vision that undergirds a unique mission, and while these stories do not add up to one narrative, some common themes emerge.

Common Themes

The first is that theological schools are the products of religion building.[14] Theological schools come into being because some form of reli-

---

13. Marsden, *Reforming Fundamentalism*, p. 54.
14. Craig Dykstra of Lilly Endowment has made this point, in several settings.

gion is growing or emerging. For St. Mary's it was an effort to educate a national priesthood for an immigrant church in a newly formed nation. For Emmanuel, it was to provide the theological education that a newly merged denomination deserved, in service to a national church. For Virginia Union, it was to bring education to freed slaves, who under slavery could be punished for knowing how to read the Bible. For Fuller, it was to bring intellectual leadership to a movement that had spent too much time in separatist and narrowly sectarian squabbles. The stories are different, but what is common is that some form of religion was emerging or growing in each.

The second common theme is that theological schools serve similar purposes. While schools have typically been founded for many reasons, most have included among those reasons the education of religious leaders and, in one way or another, the intellectual support for a growing religious community. It varies of course. For Roman Catholics, a teaching magisterium determines the content of Catholic doctrine, which makes the intellectual work of faculty at St. Mary's different from the work at Fuller, which was founded to become a kind of teaching magisterium for Evangelical Protestants. Intellectual leadership was never a problem for the early twentieth-century Vanderbilt Biblical Department, but when the Methodists bolted, the school had to redefine the communities for which it would educate religious leaders.

The third is that theological schools are frequently associated with religious controversy. For St. Mary's, it was concern about the resources that a seminary would consume. For Virginia Union, it was the Civil War, the greatest conflict in American history, and the need for religious leadership for freed but poor and socially marginalized African Americans. For Emmanuel, it was the sad reality that the formation of a national Protestant church was fractured by the failure of the Presbyterian Church, as a whole, to enter the merger. For Vanderbilt, it was conflict over governance and church control. For Fuller, it was responding to a controversy that had embraced early twentieth-century Protestantism. When church bodies split or unite, theological schools embody the stress and struggle, and sometimes, new schools are formed.

A fourth common theme is that theological schools are value-driven institutions. Religion is about issues of ultimate concern, and even small discussions in theological schools can be energized by perceptions and convictions about ultimate issues. In a seminary, both sides of a debate usually claim the high moral ground. Seminaries are environments that nurture value and meaning and, by so doing, invite unique loyalties, commitments, and sometimes, controversies.

In their varying and particular ways, most theological schools in North America trace their beginnings to some religious movement, have existed to educate religious leaders and lend intellectual support to the work of churches and denominations, encountered their share of controversy, and functioned throughout their histories as schools driven by values and issues of ultimate importance. These common characteristics provide a sufficient basis for a case for theological schools as a whole, even though the case needs to be redacted in unique ways for each school.

Critiques of Theological Schools

Theological schools, particularly Protestant schools, have been pursued by critique and worry. The Methodists were not sure whether theological education was going to hurt or help Methodist piety in the South, and the founders of Fuller had renounced theological schools that had "gone liberal." Theological schools at the beginning of this century also have their share of critics. Some critiques are formal and carefully argued while others are more like gossip or "conventional wisdom." I have read and listened to these concerns over many years now, thought about them, and want to summarize them because the case for theological schools, in this era, must be sensitive to them.

One critique is about the impact of theological education on faith and piety. Some people worry that theological schools threaten the faithfulness of students. Many of my students in the 1970s and 1980s told me that someone had advised them, when they said they were going to seminary, "not to let seminary ruin their faith." Most candidates for ministry begin theological study for lofty reasons, often at personal sacrifice, as people of faith who perceive that God has called them. The idealism and initial commitments of new seminary students typically change during seminary, and this change can be perceived as a crisis, or even loss, of faith. Most typically, this "crisis" is a normal developmental aspect of maturing faith. Intellectually informed Christian belief differs from popular belief. Ministry is a complex and difficult form of work. It requires faith that has encountered difficult questions and learned to live through them and with them. People who equate piety with particular popular beliefs often have harsh things to say about theological schools.

Another form of this criticism is about intellectual work itself. Some people believe intellect and faith are somehow antithetical. I taught at a school related to a denomination that was in conflict most of the time I was there. One fall, the chair of the board of trustees — a graduate of our school and a supporter of the seminary and its faculty — told the faculty that it was better to be a "fool on fire than a scholar on ice." Although he was a friend and alumnus of the seminary, his rhetoric reflected a form of anti-intellectualism that often finds its way into critiques of theological schools. Given the choice of good intellectual work or passionate faith, he would prefer the latter. The problem is that this dichotomy poses a faulty contest that forces an unnecessary choice. Solid intellectual work fuels passion about what is good and true. The Christian tradition has a strong intellectual element. From the complex theological arguments in the book of Romans, to Martin Luther's intellectually rigorous commentary about Romans, to the scholarly effort necessary to translate a difficult text like Romans, intellectual work exercises a gift of God to inform and advance the faith. One definition often cited for theology is that it is "faith seeking understanding." Intellectual work is a friend of faith and stokes fires of commitment. It provides ballast for unsettling moments and understands when Mystery must be left to stand without parsing or explanation.

Another kind of complaint is a lament, and reflects the perception that, as churches and theological schools have changed over the years, something crucial and precious has been lost. Two long-term faculty members of mainline Protestant schools have written laments in the last several years. One mourns the loss of what he considers the doctrinal clarity and intellectual rigor of an earlier time. The other employs harsher language to argue that, in an effort to be open to new ideas, some seminaries have welcomed positions that many Christians would call heretical, and that the legitimate differentiation between the historic core of Christian believing and experimental edges has evaporated. Both of these critiques reflect the biblical literature of lament in which some deep pain is expressed. These laments entangle issues of mainline Protestant denominations with mainline Protestant theological schools, and leave the reader to worry that things may be so broken they cannot be fixed.[15]

It is difficult, if not impossible, for theological schools to reframe their future on the basis of these kinds of concerns. Anxieties about intellectual endeavor or laments about what can't be fixed cannot be readily addressed by theological schools. No amount of intellectual effort a school can exert will relieve concerns about intellectual work and faith. A lament is an announcement that something bad has happened. It is not a warning that the enemy is coming; it is a description of the village that already has been pillaged. Laments do not pave a way to the future.

Other kinds of critique, however, are more instructive. In fact, they may be the best possible teachers for theological schools, and if the schools are good students, they will listen. I am going to mention these concerns here, and return to them at greater length in subsequent chapters.

Serious research about theological education undertaken in the 1980s and 1990s — the Basic Issues and Issues Research projects of Lilly Endowment Inc. and The Association of Theological Schools — resulted in the most significant literature on theological education in the past seventy years.[16] The research identified what theological

15. I am referring to John H. Leith, *Crisis in the Church: The Plight of Theological Education* (Louisville, Ky.: Westminster John Knox Press, 1997) and Thomas C. Oden, *Requiem: A Lament in Three Movements* (Nashville, Tenn.: Abingdon Press, 1995).

16. This literature is far too extensive to be cited here. A brief but excellent summary of this whole area of study can be found in Barbara G. Wheeler and David H.

schools historically had done that they have ceased doing over time, what has happened to theological education as it has become increasingly influenced by North American higher education and academic guilds, and what has happened as unifying elements of the curriculum have given way to increasing specialization. It is a sustained and exceptionally well-reasoned assessment of theological education in North America, and while attempts to change the expectations and practices of theological schools have been attentive to the assessments contained in this literature, the concerns are still relevant. Over centuries, the wisdom pertaining to God that theological education had sought to imbue has increasingly become entangled in academic perceptions of knowledge and functionalist ideas about ministry. A coherent organizing principle for the theological curriculum has given way to fragmentation, and efforts to justify theological education in the context of the research university further muddied the water. This body of literature has been joined by more recent independent studies that identify similar problems but propose different solutions, and express a continuing dis-ease with the capacity of theological schools to do what needs to be done in the future.[17]

Still another concern is not so much about theological education itself as it is about access to it. Access to theological schools is limited by cost — especially student debt upon graduation — and the requirement that theological degrees be awarded at the post-baccalaureate level. As the level of educational debt that seminary graduates carry with them into ministry continues to rise, a critique has been growing that graduate, professional theological education is simply too expen-

Kelsey, "The ATS Basic Issues Research Project: Thinking about Theological Education," *Theological Education* 30, no. 2 (Spring 1994): 71-80. A comprehensive bibliography of publications related to issues in theological education, including all the articles and books that were part of the Basic Issues Research/Issues Research agenda, was initially published by the Auburn Center for the Study of Theological Education and subsequently republished in *Theological Education* 30, no. 2 (Spring 1994): 89-98.

17. An example of this more recent literature is Robert J. Banks, *Reenvisioning Theological Education: Exploring a Missional Alternative to Current Models* (Grand Rapids: Wm. B. Eerdmans, 1999) and Linda Cannell, *Theological Education Matters: Leadership Education for the Church* (Newburgh, Ind.: EDCOT Press, 2006).

sive for the level of income that many graduates are likely to attain. Theological schools provide a wonderful form of education, but unless it can be obtained without incurring a large debt load, it is unjust both to graduates who are saddled with these loans and congregations that struggle with limited resources. The baccalaureate prerequisite for admission to ATS member schools is especially a concern for two large groups. The first is older students who want to serve in ministry, but never completed a baccalaureate degree. At 55, they have ten or fifteen years to give in ministerial service, and the prospect of five or six years of education to finish college and attend seminary significantly reduces the number of years available for service. The second is the fast growing Hispanic community in the United States, which has the lowest percentage of baccalaureate holders. If theological education is only available at the post-baccalaureate level, this religiously active ethnic community will not have the religious leadership it needs.[18]

A final concern is the most crucial to the case that I will make for theological schools. It questions the continued usefulness of theological schools and the value of their current work. This concern poses the greatest danger to theological education. If theological schools are not good for meeting their primary missions, there is not much of a case to be made for their work. One version of this concern questions whether theological education is needed for the practice of ministry, and another questions whether schools are the best place for theological education to be located.

Does good ministerial work depend on advanced study in a theological school? There are, after all, many talented and able ministers who do very good work but were never seminary-trained. Do they prove that theological schools may not be needed? Is ministry like business, which has some very successful entrepreneurs and executives who graduated from collegiate business schools and others, equally successful, who never took a business course and are proud of it?

18. The Commission on Accrediting degree program standards permit as many as 10 percent of professional master's students to be admitted without the baccalaureate degree, so the question is whether the baccalaureate requirement should be modified in more substantive ways.

The subjects and skills that are learned in formal educational settings are sometimes learned without those settings. Some children learn to read without going to school, and some musicians learn to play an instrument without taking lessons. These instances, however, do not mean that schools are unnecessary. Schools provide needed instruction to a wide range of individuals, a few of whom might have learned the lessons without the school, most of whom, however, would not. Schools provide structured learning that maximizes opportunities for the widest possible range of students. Some students may not learn their lessons well, and some schools may not teach them well, but schools still offer the best opportunity for the most students to learn. A few brilliantly successful ministers who never attended seminary do not invalidate the value of school for the many brilliantly effective ministers who did. The work of ministry and priesthood needs schools because ministry is an increasingly complex task, because the education level of parishioners is rising, because the world is an increasingly complicated place, because the religious and moral dilemmas in this age are increasingly demanding, and because schools are the best setting in which the knowledge, skills, perceptions, and dispositions that are needed for this time can be learned.

Should ministerial education be located in a school or in the congregation? Some people contend that the fundamental nature of a school and the patterns of work that accrue to schools are incongruent with the fundamental nature of the church and the practices that religious leadership requires. Older forms of theological education were housed in the cathedral, where the bishop and experienced clergy oversaw the training of new ministers before they were sent to rural parishes. Some would like to reinvent the cathedral model, with more focus on Evangelical megachurches than cathedrals. Clergy education, this argument goes, would be better housed in congregations and large churches where students could learn effective models of congregational work from the churches that invented that work, much of it reflecting new paradigms of congregational practice. These critics argue that schools, as schools, become preoccupied with issues and concerns that are of limited consequence in the work of congregational ministry and are prone to the temptation to "over-teach" some things of limited value and "under-teach" other things that are essential for ministry. I will address this concern more directly in chapter 5, but a limited response is appropriate here as well.

Schools are good at teaching many things that are important for ministry. A school is a good place to learn the biblical story, its meaning, and the ancient languages in which the Bible was written. School is an excellent place to learn the history of the church and the way that the church has understood the biblical text through the centuries. School is also a very good setting to learn theology and the way that believing communities have come to understand the work and love of God in the world. Schools are formative environments, and they facilitate students being shaped as both religious leaders and faithful human beings. There are some things that are better learned in ministry settings, but that does not invalidate the rich range of subjects, skills, sensitivities, and perceptions that schools teach.

Theological schools cannot map out a viable future merely by responding to the currently expressed concerns. Removing the sources of discontent does not produce satisfaction. Concerns are good teachers, but not good designers for the future. Addressing the issues that will contribute to strengthening and improving theological schools will increase effectiveness and, perhaps, satisfaction. The case for theological schools must be built on the good that they are doing and their capacity to learn how to do what most needs to be done more effectively in the future.

The Case for Theological *Schools*

Thus far, I have used theological education and theological schools somewhat interchangeably. However, they are two different things. At an ATS meeting in the early 1990s, one participant said that eventually The Association of Theological Schools will need to determine if it wants to become The Association for Theological *Education* or remain The Association of Theological *Schools*. The comment rightly pointed out that theological education and theological schools are not the same thing. Theological education is a broad enterprise. It includes degree and non-degree programs for the education of church leaders. It includes thousands of *institutos* and training institutes for the education of pastors who have little or no college experience. It includes congregation-based programs and denominationally sponsored initiatives to educate leaders who have been or will be credentialed by alternative procedures. All of these forms of theological education are valuable, serve the church and its mission in the world, and need to continue and get better at what they are doing.

Theological schools, like the more than 250 members of the Association, are a subgroup of the broader category of theological education. They employ faculties, maintain and grow libraries, admit students to advanced programs of study, grant graduate professional and research degrees, and have endowments. The case for theological schools does not depend on devaluing other parts of the broader ecology. Rather, it emerges from the contribution that theological schools uniquely make. Theological schools bring particular strengths, make particular contributions, and provide particular benefits for communities of faith.

One asset is that theological schools are *schools,* and schools have institutional strengths. Christianity is undergoing considerable change in North America. The church needs institutions that can stand at least one step outside the fray, hold onto the long tradition, and provide wisdom that transcends the immediate need. In some ways, theological schools may need to function like monasteries did in the early medieval era: places where religious traditions are preserved, contemplated, renewed, and transmitted. Theological schools have always done some of this, and in the future, may very likely need to do more.[19] Paul Bowers, who grew up in Africa as a child of missionaries and spent a career in theological education there, said in a 2007 speech, "Theological schools form the backbone of organized evangelicalism in Af-

19. I made this point in a presentation to the faculty and board of Christian Theological Seminary. Noted missiologist Andrew Walls, whose observations are far more astute than mine, made a similar point at the International Council for Evangelical Theological Education in Chiang Mai, Thailand, in 2006, as reported by Paul Bowers in a 2007 presentation.

rica. . . . Amidst all the heady vibrancy and growth of Africa's Christian communities, but also amidst all the debilitations and disorders of this continent, the theological schools have remained linked together as beacons of steadfastness, and hope, and constructive engagement."[20] The language may be too optimistic, but the comment points precisely to the role that institutionalized theological schools can play.

Schools also have educational strengths. They develop curricula, acquire information resources, cultivate a community of teachers, and become a community of practicing theological educators, and it is these resources that make a school. A school is not a school because it has a campus and endowment. It is a school because it has artfully constructed a learning environment with carefully developed goals and expectations for learning, a curricular design carefully aimed at achieving the learning goals, and a faculty that guides students toward them.

Schools are durable. Higher education institutions are among the few in North America that date from the colonial era. As providers of education, they have demonstrated their capacity to endure over time, through major cultural shifts, as well as the ability to renew themselves as different needs and issues emerge. Theological schools are robust institutions — not in the sense that they are wealthy, but in their capacity to adapt and survive. In times of stress and change, the institutional qualities of a school give theological schools the capacity to endure, to sustain needed old methods, and to invent new ones along the way.

The Case

Given the changing realities in church and higher education that characterize the present historical moment, given the common themes that emerge from particular settings and contexts, given the complaints and concerns about theological education, and given the unique character

20. Paul Bowers, "Theological Education in Africa: Why Does It Matter?" (paper presented at the AIM-SIM Theological Education Consultation, Honeydew, South Africa, March 2007), http://www.theoledafrica.org/OtherMaterials/Files/TheologicalEducationInAfrica_WhyDoesItMatter.pdf.

of schools as a setting for theological education, what is the case for theological schools? I will summarize the case here and explore it in greater depth in subsequent chapters.

Theological schools are called to prepare leaders for religious vocation. This vocation requires persons who are faithful and knowledgeable, who understand the Christian story, who are gifted for ministry and tutored in its exercise, who understand human frailty and faithful responses to it, who understand the gospel's vision of wholeness, and who can exercise leadership to increase righteousness and justice. This kind of learning requires disciplined study, critical reflection on experience, and education aimed at cultivating an understanding of responsible life in faith. Leaders who are characterized by these qualities are not educated solely by the transmission of facts or training in practices, although both are part of it. They require educational settings with sustained, integrated, formational efforts, and when theological schools do their work wisely and well, they provide exactly this kind of education. Theological schools provide a crucial resource to communities of faith by making possible the kind of learning their leaders most need.

Theological schools are ideal settings for teaching, and the Christian tradition is a teaching tradition. Jesus was rabbi, "teacher," and his ministry has been followed by faithful persons who are teachers of the church. Theological schools, once again, are an ideal setting for the development of teachers and the exercise of the art of teaching. Seminary faculty members teach in their classes, of course, but almost all of them also serve as teachers and preachers for the church. From leading worship to adult education to writing for denominational publications to conferences and workshops, faculty members are teachers of the church, not just of the students in their classes. As centers of teaching, theological schools are crucial to the work of communities of faith.

Theological schools are called to help the church remember the past, evaluate the present, envision the future, and live faithfully in relationship to all three. Each era of the Christian tradition must identify the truest understanding of the long tradition, the most intellectually faithful Christian witness, and the most honest engagement of the culture and church. Theological schools provide an ideal context for this

kind of intellectual work. Theological research takes time, library resources, the stimulation of other researchers, the questions that students raise, and an informed understanding of a wide range of issues.
Schools provide support for all of these elements. While other settings
support intellectual work, schools — when they do their work wisely
and well — comprise one of the best possible settings for this kind of
work. As centers of faithful intellectual inquiry, schools are crucial for
the work that communities of faith need to locate the underpinnings of
their beliefs in the intellectual styles of differing historical eras.

Theological schools provide more than the sum of these three activities. When learning for religious vocation, teaching leaders, and
theological research are undertaken in close connection with each
other, over time, in communities of common interest, the result is fundamentally different than if these activities are done separately. Each
of them is improved when performed in the context of the others, and
a school provides the single context that brings them together in both
expectation and practice.

When schools do their work well, they sustain communities of faith
over time, enrich the understanding that faith seeks, provide intellectual witness on behalf of religious values, and provide the kind of education that religious vocation requires. Because they are schools — with
educational skill and institutional capacity — they can address critical
problems, make significant changes, and reinvent their function as
communities of faith undergo changes. Theological schools have
strength and skills not only to serve the present, but also to do considerable good in the future. In fact, the case for theological schools is essen-
tially about their potential to serve the future. When the Commission
on Accrediting of ATS makes a grant of accreditation to a school, it is
making a statement about the future capacity of the school to function
according to the accrediting standards. On the basis of current capacity
and performance, an accreditation decision projects performance into
the future. The case I am making is not about the roles that schools
have served well in the past, or even about the value they are providing
to the present. It is, first and foremost, a statement about the value they
can provide in the future. Schools have the skill and institutional capac-

ity to hold onto what serves their mission as well as to revise programs and structures to meet the changing needs that the future requires.

How can the unique value of theological schools — their case in this historical moment — best be demonstrated? Perhaps the most effective way would be for all of them to close, and over time, communities of faith would be able to identify by their absence the contributions that theological schools had been making.

When I was in high school, I read my first book of sermons. I grew up in the congregations that were introduced to you in the beginning of this chapter, and preaching was never based on a manuscript. Often, sermons were preached without notes — not because the preacher had memorized them but because the preacher didn't always know where the sermon was going when he started. Written sermons were a discovery to me, and the first book of sermons I read was Peter Marshall's *Mr. Jones, Meet the Master*.[21] I am quite sure that this volume had more popular than critical acclaim, but as a high school junior, I thought it was great. If I was going to preach, I wanted to preach like Peter Marshall. (I was unaware that a Midwestern twang didn't have the same effect as a Scottish brogue.) In one of those sermons, Marshall tells the story of a man in a village who tended to the spring-fed reservoir from which the village drew its water. He was a bit of a recluse, not particularly loved by others in the village. To save money, the village built a cistern and eliminated the man's job. And not long thereafter, many of the people in the village became ill. The villagers wondered what was causing the illness, and eventually traced the cause to the water supply. The water had been safe before because the man made frequent trips to the reservoir and cleaned out the waste. When the waste accumulated after his departure, it became the breeding ground for the bacteria that made people ill. No one knew the good the man was doing, or how much the community depended on it, until he was gone.

21. Peter Marshall, "Keepers of the Springs," in *Mr. Jones, Meet the Master: Sermons and Prayers*, reprinted in Catherine Marshall, *The Best of Peter Marshall* (Lincoln, Va.: Chosen Books, 1983).

Theological schools were among the first educational institutions founded in both the United States and Canada. While their earlier institutional forms were different, North American Christianity has never been without theological schools of one form or another. It is difficult to discern what part of the quality of religious life is the result of something that has always been present. If the schools all closed, the character of religious leadership and congregational work would change and, eventually, the contribution that theological schools had been making would become obvious.

The next closest demonstration would be to look at areas where theological schools have not always existed. I was at a meeting of the presidents of one hundred Protestant seminaries in Latin America, Africa, the Middle East, Eastern Europe, and Asia. All of them worked in schools that were relatively new, and many of them were working in situations of great stress. One president coaches teachers and visiting speakers to stay away from the classroom windows, because of frequent gunfire. Another runs an institution in an economy with an inflation rate in the multiple thousands. None of them has enough money. They struggle to provide theological education on continents without advanced degree programs, and all the faculty travel great distances to further their education. They are working in the majority world, where Christianity is growing fast and a young, vibrant church is asking for leaders who have been theologically educated. They are founding schools and expanding existing ones. They talked with me about the value of school-based education that provided depth and substance to the piety and enthusiasm of students and religious leaders.

I want theological schools to stay open, lively, and well because many communities of faith are already stressed, and they need the ballast that a deeply formed cadre of vocational leaders will provide. Fortunately, evidence of the value of these schools is abundant, and they need not close to demonstrate their contribution.

CHAPTER 2

The Work of Theological Schools:
Learning for Religious Vocation

I was a seminary student during the morally entangled era of the Vietnam War and the Civil Rights Movement. A pivotal moment occurred in the spring of 1970, the semester almost over. A May 4 demonstration at Kent State University protesting the American invasion of Cambodia turned tragic. Four students were killed and nine injured when the Ohio National Guard fired on the protesters. The seminary determined to have a day of prayer in response. Some professors cancelled classes; others met but devoted some time to prayer and reflection. Wayne Oates was one of the school's best-known professors, and one whom students thought was especially wise. After the bell rang, and the last few students straggled in, he looked over the lectern and said, "This has been declared a day of prayer. My son is in the Mekong Delta, on a gun boat, fighting in this war. My namesake, Wayne Barnett [son of another seminary professor] fled the country because he concluded that this is an immoral war. You tell me how to pray." He was quiet for a while, then said, "Class dismissed," and walked out the door. At first, none of the students left. We just sat quietly in our chairs. Our moral certainty was stopped in its tracks by the complexity of prayer in morally ambiguous moments. The fundamental need for humility in all prayer began to dawn on us. We left slowly, each of us at different times. I still remember that moment vividly. I was shaped by that moment, maybe even changed by it.

William Hull's course on the Teaching of Jesus had a similar effect. While no singular event stands out as it did in Oates's class, the course as a whole was a deeply formative experience. Carefully taught and consistently challenging, this course reoriented my thoughts about the core of Christian teaching. I read Rudolph Bultmann's *Jesus and the Word* and encountered Albert Schweitzer's sacred summary of the Jesus who "comes to us as One unknown, without a name, as of old, by the lake-side. . . . He speaks to us the same word: 'Follow thou me!' and sets us to the tasks which He has to fulfill for our time . . . reveals Himself in the toils, the conflicts, the sufferings . . . and, as an ineffable mystery, they shall learn in their own experience Who He is."[1] We spent a semester talking about the teaching and preaching of the Kingdom of God and its nearness when the way and will of God are observed. This course, more than any other, led me both to a more sure faith and a deeper respect for ineffable mystery. The teaching of Jesus I encountered in that course continues to teach me. It was a time when I learned in my own experience more of "Who He is," and what it means to follow him.

That same year, I took Glenn Hinson's class on the Classics of Christian Devotion. It was one of those book-a-week courses: Augustine, St. Theresa and St. John of the Cross, William Law and Thomas Kelly, Alfred Delp and Dietrich Bonhoeffer, Thomas Merton and others. We were asked to keep a journal as we read, but the more I read, the less I wanted to write. I was living into others' words. I encountered stories of faith that moved and motivated me, alarmed and troubled me. I don't remember many class discussions or lectures. I just remember reading these books as winter slowly turned to spring. Thirty-five years later, they remain in the conference room by my office, on the third shelf on the far left side. Other books on Christian spirituality have been added through the years, but the sight of these

---

1. Albert Schweitzer, *The Quest of the Historical Jesus*, trans. W. Montgomery (New York: MacMillan, 1956), p. 403.

faded covers takes me back to that spring, when I read stories of faith and found my own story being reconstructed. I finished the journal, but it consisted mostly of quotations from the readings. I had spent a semester with saints; their words formed me in ways that I could not form into words.

I have heard enough stories like these from other seminary graduates to conclude that my experiences were typical rather than exceptional. Seminary education may have its share of forgettable educational moments, but its central educational agenda is a deep and crucial form of learning. It is the soul-shaping learning that forms religious vocation.

Learning for Religious Vocation

ATS member schools share a common understanding about the intent of the theological curriculum. It has not emerged from their acceptance of a particular scholarly assessment of theological education, although it has been informed by those assessments. It has not been derived from a common understanding of what a school is or should be; ATS schools have differing perceptions about that.[2] The shared curricular understanding is the result of a process by which Roman Catholics, Evangelical Protestants, mainline Protestants, and Orthodox Christians adopted an accrediting standard on the theological curriculum. It is the only statement of its kind. Standards can be technical and bureaucratic, but this one reflects a central aspiration of theological educators.

> In a theological school, the overarching goal is the development of theological understanding, that is, an aptitude for theological reflection and wisdom pertaining to responsible life in faith.

2. David H. Kelsey, in *To Understand God Truly: What's Theological About a Theological School* (Louisville, Ky.: Westminster/John Knox Press, 1992), makes this point. If a common perception of either theology or school is necessary for a common understanding of theological schools, such an understanding would not be possible.

Comprehended in this overarching goal are others such as deepening spiritual awareness, growing in moral sensibility and character, gaining an intellectual grasp of the tradition of a faith community, and acquiring the abilities requisite to the exercise of ministry in that community.[3]

The Overarching Curricular Goal

The overarching goal of the theological curriculum is a "theological understanding," which is an "aptitude for theological reflection and wisdom pertaining to responsible life in faith." Edward Farley, in a 1980s groundbreaking study, argued that theological education needs to recover learning that contributes to a *theological habitus*. By *habitus,* he meant a sapiential and personal knowledge, the kind of knowing that disposes one toward God. The overarching goal of theological education, therefore, is a wisdom related to the ways of God.[4] The ATS standard uses the language of "understanding" with a very particular meaning. "Christian understanding," in Charles Wood's language, reflects "a whole collection of capacities and abilities that go to make up the Christian life."[5] It is informed, thoughtful, and critically engaged. It is an overarching and undergirding kind of knowing. Ministerial work requires knowledge and skills, to be sure, but skills, abilities, and knowledge are not the ultimate goal of theological education. Farley argues that the more theological education focuses on ministerial tasks, the less qualified the minister will be to perform those tasks![6] In the language of the standard, the ultimate goal of the theological curriculum is the kind of "theological reflection and wisdom pertaining to responsible life in faith."

3. Commission on Accrediting, Standard 4, "The Theological Curriculum," Section 4.1, "Goals of the Theological Curriculum."

4. Edward Farley, *Theologia: The Fragmentation and Unity of Theological Education* (Philadelphia: Fortress Press, 1983), p. 153.

5. Charles M. Wood, *The Formation of Christian Understanding: An Essay in Theological Hermeneutics* (Philadelphia: The Westminster Press, 1981), p. 23.

6. Farley, *Theologia,* p. 128.

As part of a major project in the early 1970s, The Association of Theological Schools undertook an effort to identify what clergy and laity considered either essential or detrimental to the ministerial work of recent seminary graduates. A survey was administered to a broad sample of seminary professors, pastors, denominational officials, and laypeople. The analysis of the responses to hundreds of questions by thousands of people concluded that, at the most global level, people tend to assess the work of ministers and priests in terms of three broad questions: Do they truly love God? Do they relate with care and integrity to human beings? Do they have the knowledge and skills that the job requires?[7] As best I can tell, these three questions continue to hold true. Not only do people tend to ask them, they tend to ask them in this order. If the answer to the first question is "no," people don't even proceed to the second or third questions. If they are convinced that a minister or priest does not know or love God, they have little interest in how well that person preaches, administers, counsels, or how much propositional theology or biblical content he or she knows.

"Does a minister or priest love God?" is not the same as the "theological understanding" in the accrediting standards, but the two concepts are deeply compatible. Learning for religious vocation does not begin with the mastery of various skill sets or acquisition of technical religious information. It begins with learning to be *Christian*: truly, deeply, thoughtfully, intelligently, lovingly, Christian. This is a wonderfully appropriate curricular goal and a breathtakingly difficult educational task. This aptitude is nurtured partly by a student's educational sweat and tears, partly as a gift of the Spirit, and partly by the

7. This is an extrapolation of the findings of factor analysis of the survey results; see Daniel Aleshire's chapter in Merton Strommen, David Schuller, and Milo Brekke, *Ministry in America* (New York: Harper and Row, 1980). The Profiles of Ministry survey was initially administered in 1973; then administered again in 1988; then administered a third time in 2003. The ratings of importance of these ministerial characteristics have changed very little over this thirty-year period. See Francis Lonsway, "Profiles of Ministry: History and Current Research," *Theological Education* 41, no. 2 (2006); "The Churches and the Preparation of Candidates for Ministry," *Theological Education* 42, no. 1 (2006); and "What's in an Instrument? The Answer from the Profiles of Ministry Program," *Theological Education* 42, no. 2 (2007).

work of faculty and mentors. It is not the sort of learning that can be addressed as a course objective, nor is it the sort of learning that easily lends itself to observable outcomes. This is learning that does not cease at the conclusion of seminary. It is learning for religious vocation.

How does this kind of learning take place in a theological school? It begins with the serious, critical study of sacred texts. The Truth to which the texts point is infinitely sturdy and readily stands up to critical inquiry. Learning that leads to theological understanding requires studying the history of believing communities and the literature in which faith seeks reason that gives form and structure to believing. This kind of learning also requires worship and prayer, service and witness. "Wisdom pertaining to responsible life in faith" is a personal, intellectually rigorous, experiential knowledge. Seminaries put it on display every once in a while, as happened that day in Professor Oates's class, and they create the settings in which it is perceived, like reading St. John of the Cross one rainy, cold week in March. Perhaps most importantly, this kind of learning emerges from engagement with people who are teaching and learning together, which is why the accrediting standards require students to have at least some face-to-face contact with faculty and other students during the course of their studies.

Seminary education is not about texts on the one hand and people on the other. Often, faculty members become the most important texts their students read. Kenneth Mulholland was dean and professor at Columbia Biblical Seminary in South Carolina. He was a missionary pastor and strategist, and he had the capacity to care equally about individuals and the world's people as a whole. He was, if I ever met one, "an Israelite in whom there is no guile." I think he taught in ways that invited students not just to thinking about missionary strategy but also to theological understanding. He died several years ago after a debilitating bout with cancer, and the last thing I read that he wrote was his final family Christmas letter. His grandson was also being treated for cancer, and his Advent hope was in his grandson's cure. Wisdom pertaining to responsible life in faith is substantive, without cliché. Timothy Lull died while recovering from surgery. At the time, he was president at Pacific Lutheran Theological Seminary and a Luther scholar. I think Tim was a bit like Luther, at least as I imagine Luther to have been, brilliant and devoted. Tim may have had more tenderness and less torment than the Reformer, but he was no less a theologian or lover of the church. He wrote an imaginative book[8] not long before he died that recorded mythical conversations with Luther. The most memorable for me was the one where Tim and Luther are walking back from the site of a German concentration camp. Tim asks Luther about his comments about the Jews, and if he thought there was any link between what he said and what Nazi Germans did. Luther responds with a bit of an explanation, but in the end, surrenders to the ambiguity of human failure. Tim taught and administered as one seeking theological understanding.

These people, in their own ways, did not merely teach the theological curriculum, they *became* the curriculum. In them, there was a "wisdom pertaining to responsible life in faith." They had studied hard for years and grappled with ideas and texts, and in the end, they had more than the sum of the intellectual work they had done — Christianity's hopes and longings had taken up residence in them. The theological curriculum does not consist merely of courses and degree requirements. Perhaps more importantly, it consists of teachers and others who so embody theological wisdom that they form a cloud of witnesses who have become texts worthy of study. Theological schools are full of faculty like these.

Curricular Elements within the Overarching Goal

The overarching goal of theological education is unitary, but like white light refracted by a prism, the overarching goal can be refracted into its elements.

Learning for religious vocation involves "deepening spiritual awareness" and growth in "moral sensibility and character." When

8. Timothy F. Lull, *My Conversations with Martin Luther* (Minneapolis: Augsburg, 1999).

the current ATS accrediting standards were proposed, discussed, and finally approved, these two phrases drew a lot of attention. No one discounted the value of deepened spiritual awareness or moral sensibility for ministry, but there were questions about whether it was the responsibility of a theological school to focus its efforts on these needed aspects or whether another context, such as the church, should be the center for this kind of formation. By including these statements in the accrediting standards, the schools accepted at least some responsibility for addressing these issues and, with this acceptance, education takes on a different character. A student does not learn principles of spirituality and then apply them to spiritual life. Rather, a student grows in spiritual awareness. A student does not learn moral principles and then apply them in life. There is often considerable distance from the good that people know they should do and the good that they actually do. Students will not graduate spiritually or morally mature — these are lifelong tasks for people of faith — but the language of the standard requires schools to accept responsibility for nurturing growth in these areas.

Learning for religious vocation requires "gaining an intellectual grasp of the tradition of the faith community." Schools have always been very good at this task, and are most confident about student learning in this area. The schools both know how to teach subjects like church history and biblical languages and how to assess student learning in them. Students learn the biblical text and how to interpret it, theology and how doctrine has emerged historically, and the history of the long tradition in which their faith is located. The Auburn Center for the Study of Theological Education completed a survey of Master of Divinity (M.Div.) graduates of ATS member schools who had been out of seminary between five and ten years. When asked how important each of several major areas of study has been to their professional life and work, survey respondents made "biblical studies" their top choice, followed by theology. This was true for Roman Catholic, mainline Protestant, and Evangelical Protestant graduates. These areas of study are crucial to learning for religious vocation, but have been erroneously termed the "classical disciplines." Ministerial leaders cannot function without a deep understanding of the tradition of the faith community, but if that is all they have, they may not be able to function very well at all.

Learning for religious vocation also requires "acquiring the abilities requisite to the exercise of ministry in that community." These abilities include preaching, liturgical arts, teaching, counseling, administration, congregational and community analysis, evangelization, community organizing and public witness, and other aspects of ministerial practice. Religious vocation involves the exercise of a wide range of activities, and theological schools seek to maximize the quality with which these practices are performed. These activities are not the "applied" version of what is learned more "theoretically" in biblical or theological studies. Preaching and teaching are ways that biblical truth and theological constructs are communicated, but they are not applications of that truth.

Given all this, what is learning for religious vocation? It is the development of theological understanding that relates to responsible life in faith. This understanding is not the result of acquiring knowledge in different subject areas or accumulating different educational experiences. It is not knowledge about God; it is learning that results in knowing God. Wisdom pertaining to responsible life in faith is not the exclusive domain of ordained clergy or religious professionals. It is a wisdom to which all people of faith can aspire. The goal of theological learning is not the accrual of ever greater amounts of religious knowledge; it is the transformation of learners into different kinds of Christian believers.

Perspectives on Theological Learning

The overarching goal of theological learning permeates the work of theological schools. The educational task of these schools, however, extends in many directions and can be understood from a variety of perspectives. Each of these perspectives provides insight and, of course, each raises questions about the educational agenda in theological education.

Learning between Athens and Berlin

Learning for religious vocation draws from two very different models — both imported from Europe — for understanding the aims and purposes of higher education in North America. These have been identified by David Kelsey as "Athens" and "Berlin."[9]

The Athens tradition predates Christianity and reflects the Greek vision of education as *paideia. Paideia,* as Kelsey abstracts this broad educational philosophy, is a kind of education that, among other things, seeks to cultivate excellence of the soul, which consists "in knowledge of the Good itself." This knowledge "requires a conversion, a turning around of the soul from preoccupation with appearances to focus on reality, on the Good." As Christians worked with the educational ideal of *paideia,* the focus shifted to the kind of education that prepared persons "for inward and religious transformation."[10] The Athens model was the dominant educational model in the development of medieval English universities and continued to influence English and European universities through the eighteenth century. It is very much in evidence in theological education as students not only learn the subject matter, but also grow in spiritual maturity. They graduate both knowing the Christian story and being more congruent and faithful Christians. Much of the discussion in the previous section of this chapter was about the necessity and value of the "Athens" kind of learning.

The more recent educational model has its roots in the nineteenth-century foundation of the University of Berlin. Instead of a focus on *paideia,* the Berlin pattern focused on rationality and critical inquiry. In this tradition, inquiry is "*critical* in that it begins by requiring justification of all alleged authorities or bases of truth . . . *disciplined* in the sense that it is highly self-conscious about the methods that are used to establish the truth . . . [and] *orderly* in that it seeks to locate its subject matter in the context of the largest possible set of relations to other

---

9. David H. Kelsey, *Between Athens and Berlin: The Theological Education Debate* (Grand Rapids: William B. Eerdmans Publishing Company, 1993).

10. Kelsey, *Between Athens and Berlin,* pp. 9-10.

things."[11] The Berlin model has limited room for truth derived from revelation or for any kind of student formation other than critical intellectual formation. As a result, the founders of the University of Berlin questioned whether a university oriented to this educational philosophy could even have a divinity school. Berlin did include a divinity school, but in order to do so, invented a new pattern of ministerial education, refocused on two elements: orderly, critical research and "professional" education for ministry. In this model, students learn how to engage critically the subject matter, develop the ability to pursue truth in self-critical and disciplined ways, learn to make rational and coherent cases for what they think is true, and develop critical professional skills.

These two traditions represent very different educational goals, and they are deeply present in current higher education practices. My son graduated from what I think is a good liberal arts institution. His school participates in a program that seeks to "instill in students an abiding sense of social responsibility and civic concern." The program uses engaged learning "to prepare students 'to be global citizens and informed leaders motivated by concern for the common good.'"[12] That is *paideia* education. As best I can tell from the reports that made it back home, my son consistently encountered rhetoric and practices that valued learning for leadership on behalf of a common good. I know that this school wants baccalaureate graduates who are rational, critical thinkers, but from what I have heard two states away, it appears that this institution would think its most successful graduates were ones who have learned to become "informed leaders motivated by a common good." This is higher education in the *paideia* model.

By contrast, most faculty members in ATS schools completed their Ph.D.'s in research universities. For theological studies to have a place in these kinds of institutions, they needed to follow the model that was invented at the University of Berlin. While Ph.D. degree programs may have rhetoric that values graduates becoming responsible, value-

---

11. Kelsey, *Between Athens and Berlin*, pp. 13-14.
12. www.elon.edu/community/pericles.

oriented professors, the bottom line in many of those programs is that graduates know a subject area extraordinarily well, are able to engage it critically and argue it rationally, and have the capacity to engage in critical research that advances understanding and knowledge. If students learn to be good persons along the way, that would be nice, but would not substitute for the critical skills and abilities that constitute the virtues of the Berlin model. Higher education has a tendency to denominate itself along these lines. Liberal arts institutions tend to emphasize the learning associated with Athens and graduate schools and research universities emphasize the learning associated with Berlin.

Theological schools, however, deeply identify with both educational models. Both are present in the ATS accrediting standards. In a 2003 survey of ATS faculty conducted by the Auburn Center, more faculty identified "critical thinking" as the most hoped for outcome of their teaching than any other option given.[13] The next most hoped for outcome was integration. The first is straight from Berlin and the second tips its hat toward Athens. Faculties want both. Kelsey notes, however, that "The two models sit together very uneasily. The tension between them is never resolved, and no theological school escapes struggles created by the tension between them." Kelsey thinks that there can only be "negotiated truces."[14] In their study of clergy education in the United States, researchers at the Carnegie Foundation for the Advancement of Teaching noted Kelsey's points about Athens and Berlin, and they interviewed faculty about how they dealt with both goals. One professor at a university divinity school said that he hoped students would discover how to "combine loyalty and criticism, devotion and creativity."[15] An Old Testament professor at an Evangelical seminary said that he does not want students "to have one part of their

---

13. Barbara G. Wheeler, Sharon L. Miller, and Katarina Schuth, "Signs of the Times: Present and Future Theological Faculty," *Auburn Studies,* no. 10 (February 2005).

14. Kelsey, *Between Athens and Berlin,* p. 92.

15. Charles R. Foster, Lisa E. Dahill, Lawrence A. Goleman, and Barbara Wang Tolentino, *Educating Clergy: Teaching Practices and Pastoral Imagination* (San Francisco: Jossey-Bass, 2006), p. 48.

brain that works critically and then another part that works devotion-
ally."[16] I think that most theological faculties want their students to
learn in both of these ways so that they graduate as Christian human
beings who think critically and rationally.

Other cities vie for inclusion in the geography of theological learning. Kelsey suggests that the map might include cities that were centers
of religious movements — like Jerusalem and Rome in Christianity's
earliest days, and Wittenberg and Geneva during the Reformation.
The religious impulses that emerged in particular moments are com-
mingled with educational impulses in theological education practices.
Newer locations are exercising a growing influence on North American theological schools. Silicon Valley deserves mention, with the
enormous impact that technology is having on religious practices,
availability of information, and patterns of higher education. Nairobi
and Seoul are important to add as Christianity grows in the Global
South and Asia, and by so doing, repositions Christianity in the West.
While these and other cities will contribute to the educational agenda
of the future, the two impulses that Kelsey identified as Athens and
Berlin will continue to influence theological education.

Professional Learning, Academic Learning, and Personal Learning

Learning in theological schools has historically been intended for two
different vocational uses, either professional ministry or academic
mastery. A third use is emerging, and it involves personal learning for
understanding. The preparation for each of these is similar in terms of
subjects studied and educational process; the difference is in intended
use after graduation.

A professional theological degree is intended to be used in some
form of the practice of ministry, and an academic degree is intended to
be used for subject mastery or further academic study. Theological study
for personal understanding is most often undertaken by laypersons who

16. Foster et al., *Educating Clergy*, p. 48.

have no intention to enter ministerial work or undertake further academic pursuits. Professional theological degrees, like the Master of Divinity, parallel higher education degrees in social work, physical or occupational therapy, teaching, marriage and family therapy, and counseling. Most of these professions require post-baccalaureate education, typically a professional master's or doctoral degree, and they equip people with the specialized skills that these professions require. Graduate academic degrees in theology, like a Master of Arts in Biblical Studies, parallel higher education degrees like a Master of Arts in History, or English, or Philosophy. These degrees provide advanced knowledge in these subject areas, but do not qualify persons for particular jobs, except teaching or researching in these subject areas. Personal learning for understanding has increased in theological education as well as in higher education in general. These programs of study are not necessarily required for current employment but provide an intellectually rich understanding of some area. In theological studies, these programs of study may be pursued because persons hope to serve more effectively as lay leaders in their congregations, or because they have wanted to learn about their faith in a serious and advanced way. Learning for understanding, learning because one wants to know and value learning, may be the purest form of learning. It is learning for learning's sake.

The most typical uses of theological learning are either in professional ministry or academic pursuits. The difference in the two kinds of degrees has more to do with intended use than with the courses that are included in the degree program. Historically, freestanding seminaries offered only professional degrees. While university-related divinity schools offered only professional degrees, their faculties typically participated in academic degree programs that were offered through the university's graduate school. In fact, universities still regulate the distinction between academic and professional degrees by their structures. Across the past thirty years, freestanding theological schools have begun offering academic degree programs, in addition to the expansion of professional degree offerings.

The differentiation between professional and academic degrees has been getting muddier. For the most part, the same faculty provides instruction for both kinds of degree programs and many of the same courses can be credited to either kind of degree. The ATS standard on curriculum discussed at the beginning of this chapter relates to both kinds of programs. While it was written primarily with professional degree programs in mind, it has applicability to academic programs as well. For example, one would hope that advanced study of the biblical text in an academic master's program would still contribute to a theological understanding related to responsible life in faith. The Bible is still the Bible, and it has a formative power on those who perceive it as an expression of divine revelation. The results of learning for professional ministry and learning for academic study of a theological discipline become blurred.

The accrediting standards have attempted to clarify the lines in technical ways. For example, the standards require field experience or other context-based learning as a part of any professional degree program, but exclude these kinds of learning experiences from academic programs. This effort, however, is less than satisfying. Some schools, for example, offer an academic master's degree in spiritual direction. Students learn about Christian spirituality, including its theological and psychological dimensions, and they learn about the history and function of spiritual direction in the life of the church and individual Christian growth. Theoretically, graduates of this program would be qualified to teach about Christian spirituality in an undergraduate institution, but not to function as spiritual directors. Other schools offer a professional master's degree in spiritual direction. The course requirement in this degree program will include everything that is in the academic master's degree and, in addition, courses and clinical instruction in the practice of spiritual direction. Theoretically, graduates of these programs would be qualified to function as spiritual directors and, while they may teach about this Christian practice, their primary role is serving as directors, not teaching about it. The academic-professional distinction is based on an educational assumption that the nature of learning to function in a complex role is different from learning the various subjects that inform that role. The wall between these two kinds of theological learning, however, is paper-thin.

The faculties at some ATS schools have become increasingly convinced that theological learning of any kind requires both the learning that the standards associate with academic degrees and the learning associated with professional degrees. These schools would argue that a subject like spiritual direction can't be learned academically without engaging in the practice, and that it can't be learned for practice without the academic foundation. The professional and academic study of the Bible poses a similar problem. The pastor needs to know the biblical story, the nature of inspiration, how the text came into being and the history of its transmission from the ancient to the modern world, the nature of biblical languages, how the text has been interpreted in the past and present, *and* how the text is used in worship, preaching, and teaching. The lay student who wants to learn the Bible for academic study needs to learn the biblical story, the nature of inspiration, how the text came into being and the history of its transmission from the ancient to the modern world, the nature of biblical languages, and how the text has been interpreted in the past and present. Some would argue, however, that the student in the academic program cannot truly learn the biblical text without teaching it to a group and attending to their reception and questions about the text. Again, the wall between these kinds of learning is paper-thin.

Even thin walls can serve important purposes, however. Ministry is a practice, and the intellectual resources that practices require are different from the intellectual resources that the academic study of a subject requires. This is true of other practices, as well. Peter Gomes recounts his experience of hearing Yo-Yo Ma play when he was an undergraduate at Harvard.[17] It was no typical undergraduate recital. There was intelligence, even genius, in his playing. Even if Yo-Yo Ma is not the world's greatest musicologist or music theorist, few would contest the exquisite intellectual work of his playing. Just as playing music requires different intellectual resources than studying the theory of music, pastoral work requires a different kind of intellectual engagement

---

17. Peter J. Gomes, *The Good Life: Truths that Last in Times of Need* (New York: HarperSanFrancisco, 2003), p. 60.

than writing systematic theology. Not only does practice require different intellectual effort, some indicators suggest that it requires multiple kinds of intellectual effort, and the difference between superior and inferior pastoral work is that good pastors combine social, emotional, and intellectual patterns of intelligence in the practices of effective pastoral leadership. Professionally focused education seeks to attend to all the ways that ministerial practitioners need to learn. It is not clear what will happen to this educational assumption in the future. The professional/academic differentiation is dominant in higher education, but one may question if it will remain so in theological education. Theological schools serve the church, and if the church would benefit from a less rigid distinction between the two forms of education, a little baptismal water sprinkled on a paper wall just could bring it down!

While the practices of professional education remain uniquely valuable for the education of clergy and lay professional ministers, seminaries struggle with professional education more than academic education. Why? One reason is that some faculty members understand (and value) academic education more than professional education. Even if they have an M.Div. or other professional degree, most of them were educated in research doctoral programs that define top-of-the-line academic degrees. As crucial as the idea of different patterns of intellectual work appears to be, we still know less about the intellectual patterns associated with excellence in pastoral practice than we know about the intellectual patterns associated with the study of theology or the Bible.

Another reason is related to questions raised by the word "professional." Much of the twentieth century was spent establishing clergy education as a form of professional education. Some Christians worry that "professional" is an inappropriate understanding of ministerial practice. They are inclined to think that ministers are qualified if they have been called by God (and in that call given the gifts they need for ministerial leadership) and are deeply committed Christians. Others think that "professional" is so associated with a fee-for-service model — like fees to the attorney or physician — that the term has become inappropriate for the kind of work that pastors and seminary gradu-

43

ates do in communities of faith. Still others believe that the term "professional" has simply run its course as a way to understand the work of seminary-educated ministers and priests. The term has become so diffuse (from professional athlete who plays for pay, to professional tradesperson who is considered professional because the person is especially good) that it has less meaning than it once did.

Perhaps the most serious question about the professional theological education of ministers and priests is if ministry is even a profession, in the twentieth-century sense of that word. An occupational class is considered to be professional on the basis of several requirements, including: advanced (typically post-baccalaureate) education, specialized knowledge and ability, some formal process by which persons are approved, accountability for continuing professional education, and responsibility to a code of ethics and conduct established by the profession. These requirements are met by ministry in many denominations, but not all. Even in the mainline Protestant denominations where the requirements for ministry most reflect the normative requirements for profession, alternative credentialing procedures that do not reflect these requirements have been developed and continue to expand. This growing practice makes distinguishing one group as "professional" (that is, seminary-educated and working full-time in midsized and larger congregations) from a "non-professional" group that does the same thing, only part-time in smaller congregations and without a seminary education, very problematic. Theological schools may have had too limited a view of the nature of professional education. The tendency has been to focus professional education on the functions associated with the practice of ministry. Current research suggests that a much more important aspect of professional education is the formation of persons in the perceptions, habits, and sensitivities that characterize the work of the profession, not just the necessary skills or abilities. Education for ministry is an intensively formational pattern of learning, and this may emerge as the best understanding of professional education. If this understanding were to become dominant, worries and complaints about professional education for religious vocation would dissipate.

Learning for Religious Leadership

Earlier in this chapter, I followed Edward Farley's lead by arguing that theological education should not be associated only with the education of clergy and religious professionals. Theological understanding is not the exclusive domain of these leaders, and if all these leaders have learned are the skills and knowledge that religious leadership requires, they likely would not be fit for this service. However, the majority of students in theological schools in North America are studying for ministry professions, and theological schools need to attend closely to their education. In many, if not all, ways, theological education is leadership education.

One of the most enduring conundrums in theological education involves discerning which educational practices help students learn to engage the various arts of ministry. Some schools have sought to identify the entire range of ministry arts, then educate toward competence in all of them. The results have not been very positive. Students are overwhelmed with the range of practices, and either become good at none of them or seek excellence in one at the expense of the others. The problem with being good at none of them is obvious, if you have ever been around a good-hearted but inept minister. The problem with being good at only one is that most M.Div. graduates who serve in congregational ministry are solo pastors, and responsible practice requires them to use a range of ministry arts. The choice to be good at preaching and careless about administration will be problematic for their congregations.

How are the practices of ministry understood and how are they learned? Is there an organizing principle for all the functions of ministry, or do they remain a list of skill sets that require separate forms of mastery? To put it another way, are these various abilities oriented toward a common purpose? I think so, and that purpose is religious leadership. I believe that *theological* education for ministry is *leadership* education. Theological schools educate persons who, soon after they graduate, go to congregations, parishes, or nonprofit organizations and, in one form or another, exercise leadership. This is not generally the case with medical education, legal education, or graduate liberal arts education — the fields that theological schools often claim as cousins. In most other professions, leadership positions emerge over time. New graduates engage in clerkships, internships, residencies, or hold junior practitioner status before eventually advancing to leadership positions. One of the most unique characteristics of theological education is that graduates go *immediately* into positions of leadership upon graduation, if not before. The organizations they lead may be small, but from week one, the new pastor in a parish or program director in an organization is expected to lead.

Leadership has received a lot of attention in recent years. In fact, an entire academic field has grown up around it. A rich reservoir of managerial and psychological literature has been written for understanding leadership. This literature, however, does not provide a theological resource for understanding leadership in communities of faith and, as a result, leadership gets a lot of bad press around theological schools. I have heard conversations that associate leadership with autocratic or dictatorial patterns, making leadership theologically suspect. Some associate leadership with masculine patterns of work and find it troublesome to more gender-inclusive perceptions of ministry. Others perceive leadership as limiting the power of the community, rather than empowering it. These critiques notwithstanding, I would argue that good ministry is about the exercise of leadership in communities of faith. Leadership in this context needs to be understood theologically, and I'd like to identify three characteristics that are important in ministerial leadership.

First, leadership is a *function of community*, not of individuals. A violinist playing a solo does not need a conductor but an orchestra playing a symphony does. Leadership is necessary when the task to be completed is attainable only by the work of a community. The literature I have seen on leadership focuses a great deal on the attributes, skills, and characteristics of leaders. These are very important, but attention also needs to be given to the vocation of the community, the community's responsibility for nurturing leaders, and the community's responsibility to function as a lead-able ensemble.

Second, the *vocation of the community* is what counts most. Leadership is an instrumental activity, a necessary resource for the community to accomplish its calling. Leaders help a community do its work in three ways: they remind the community of its vocation — why it exists; they give organizational coherence and direction to the community, enabling the vocation to translate into concrete tasks; and they help the community find resources to fulfill its vocation, i.e. the talents and treasure it requires. Leadership is not a function of individuals who need to be in charge of something; it is a function of communities that need leaders to help them do the job they are called to do. Leadership is about empowering and guiding the community to fulfill its calling.

The third characteristic of ministerial leadership focuses on how it is practiced. Because leadership is exercised differently in different contexts, I will focus on parish leadership. Pastors lead by their preaching, teaching, administrative attention to the congregation's work, and their care of souls. These activities help the congregation identify and remember its mission, motivate the community to undertake the work it needs to do, and help the congregation find the resources it needs to fulfill its calling. A minister does not preach in order to lead, but preaching is an act of leadership. A priest does not teach in order to lead, but likewise teaching is an act of leadership. Preaching and teaching occur because something about faith, or Scripture, or the tradition, needs to be said and needs to be heard. The exercise of the normative activities of pastoral work becomes an act of leadership.

A Concluding Word about Learning for Religious Vocation

I have discussed learning in terms of the more abstract language of "theological understanding," in terms of learning that focuses on identity and character (Athens) and learning that focuses on critical assessment and technical professional skill (Berlin), in terms of learning focused on academic mastery, learning for professional practice of ministry, and, in this latter area, theological education as leadership education. In some ways, these are different dimensions of learning that contribute to a common religious vocation; and in other ways, they direct common dimensions of vocation into different patterns of learning. What is the learning, in the end, that results from these complex educational processes that occur over time, in relationship to texts, situations, contexts, and persons who form a community of faith?

I will go back to where I began. Learning for religious vocation occurs when students develop "theological understanding, that is, an aptitude for theological reflection and wisdom pertaining to responsible life in faith." Within this, students have "learned" for priesthood or ministry when they have deepened spiritual awareness, grown in moral sensibility and character, gained an intellectual grasp of the tradition of a faith community, and acquired the abilities requisite to the exercise of ministry in that community. Is there a good name for what this kind of learning enables a pastor to do? Craig Dykstra of Lilly Endowment has offered one: "pastoral imagination." Among many qualities that characterize pastoral imagination are "knowing 'how to interpret Scripture and tradition in contemporary life,' developing 'an accurate sense of what makes human beings tick,' possessing 'a complex understanding of how congregations and other institutions actually work,' and having both a 'clear awareness' and an 'analytical understanding of the world that the church exists to serve.'" All of these capacities are undergirded by a "clarity of mind about what it means to worship God in spirit and in truth."[18] In many ways, these characteristics reflect the elements that inhere in the broad concept of "theological understanding." Pastoral imagination adds a valuable dimension by suggesting that theological learning needs to be implemented in intelligently creative ways, rather than rationally wooden ways that reflect the learning but not wisdom about its implementation.

Theological schools, when they do their work well, are about the only kind of institution that make this kind of learning possible. There

18. Foster et al., *Educating Clergy*, p. 22.

48

is no more central case for school-based theological education. Learning for religious vocation engages head *and* heart, knowledge *and* skill, community faith *and* personal commitment, intellectual *and* practical wisdom, academic *and* devotional understanding. It takes a theological school to cultivate the full range of learning that religious vocation requires.

Assessing Learning for Religious Vocation

I have focused this chapter on learning for religious vocation. Had this same chapter been written twenty-five years ago, I imagine it would have been written from the perspective of *teaching* for religious vocation. Higher education is in the middle of a significant change regarding the determination of quality. The change is not complete, but it is deeply in process. The shift is not so much replacing the criteria by which judgments are made about higher education as it is adding new criteria and reweighting existing ones. The older criteria for assessing higher education focused on the quality of educational resources and processes. Good schools had well-qualified faculties, strong libraries, attractive and good facilities, talented students, and effective institutional processes. While the schools existed primarily so students could learn, the quality of the institution was measured by its resources. The newer criteria focus on the quality of student learning. Resources have not ceased to be important, but they no longer can be considered the primary indicator of educational quality. The primary indicator is student learning. The change is so significant that it is best understood as a paradigm shift.

The older paradigm focused on the *quality of teaching and accountability of learners*. When I joined a seminary faculty many decades ago, the school was implementing an evaluation procedure in which students evaluated courses, and the summary of the course evaluations were used to evaluate professors. The dominant assumption was that good teaching would create the possibility of good learning. The school was accountable for making sure the teaching was good, and students were accountable for learning. If teaching was good, failure to learn was understood as a student failure. A seminary could consider itself a good school on the basis of a competent and well-regarded faculty. The emerging paradigm focuses on *quality of learning and accountability of teachers.* If students are not learning, then, in some way or the other, the faculty is failing. The faculty may be wonderful teachers; the library may have a wonderful collection; the classrooms may have smart boards; but if students are not learning, these resources don't count for much.

The tension between teaching and learning that is drawn here is, of course, too sharp and distinct. Charles Foster, the senior researcher on the *Educating Clergy* project, used to tell his students that "when teachers teach and students learn, students teach and teachers learn." He admits to the potential shortcoming of the statement, but is right to point out that teaching and learning are not technical transactions. Teachers and learners are human beings and, therefore, teaching and learning are relational activities. When researchers in the *Educating Clergy* study asked students which aspects of teaching prompted their learning, they were intrigued "with the extent to which students said that they sought to 'imitate' faculty whom they identified as mentors — especially in the early stages of their theological education." Novice students "were more dependent on the quality of teaching," but as the students increased in their own expertise, "they became more engaged in the quality of learning." At the same time the most effective teachers tended to be most aware of and responsive to the learning impulses of their students. Teaching and learning are connected, relational activities.

However, the emerging paradigm would hold that failure of students to learn is an institutional failure. While teachers and learners share in the relational processes of education, the assessment paradigm makes teachers accountable for good learning instead of students accountable for good teaching. Students need to study, of course, and do their part, but if learning fails to occur, an institution can no longer think of itself as a "good" school. The definition of educational integrity is shifting. As the paradigm shifts and learning becomes weighted as the most important single factor in determining educational quality, the ability to assess learning becomes crucial for institutions. As best I can tell, people are more comfortable with the emphasis on learning than they are with the assessment, especially theological educators.

Like other higher education phenomena, the focus on assessment has been heavily influenced by external factors. It started with public elementary and secondary education, and its energy came primarily from state government agencies, not from local school districts or teachers. For the past twenty years the focus on student learning has descended on higher education, and once again, the most forceful impetus has been external. In the United States, the primary force has been the federal government. Since the 1980s, accrediting agencies have been regulated in ways that expect them to require the institutions they accredit to demonstrate that they are assessing the learning of their students. The regulation of accrediting standards related to assessment continues to increase, and each regulatory iteration requires ever more precise and demanding evidence that students have learned what the schools say they should learn. Failure of an accrediting agency to address educational effectiveness will lead to withdrawal of recognition by the U.S. Secretary of Education, and without that recognition, the agency's accreditation does not provide the eligibility that schools need to participate in the federally guaranteed student loan program. The ATS Commission on Accrediting is one of these recognized agencies, and federal influence is strong and getting stronger in theological education in the United States.

In addition to external factors that are forcing theological schools to assess learning more carefully, theological schools should want to assess student learning for internal reasons as well. In every course that I taught as a professor, I devoted considerable time to assessment. Tests, papers, projects, and other activities were required in each course, and I hoped that these activities would both facilitate and help me assess student learning. Like most seminaries, the last week of each semester was devoted exclusively to assessment: final exams. Combined with other tests or assessment-oriented class sessions, my students probably averaged two weeks out of every semester — almost 15 percent of their class time — in assessment activities. No one was making me do it. There was no institutional requirement that it had to be done. So why did I and my colleagues do it?

Several reasons informed the practice; I'll mention two. Theological educators care about the subjects they teach, and assessment is a way of encouraging students to learn the material. No one subject is as important to ministry as all professors think their own courses are, but they shouldn't be teaching if they don't believe their area is crucial to ministry. Most theological educators also care about the people and institutions their students will serve as graduates. Most every professor, at one time or another, has looked at his or her students and asked, "Would I want this student to be my mother's or children's pastor?" Assessment — the tasks related to sorting out the students who seem to be "getting it" from those who are not — is an expression of care for the institutions and settings in which graduates will serve.

Theological faculty have always assessed students, usually extensively, and typically for good reasons. The assessment movement, however, has been greeted with a great deal of suspicion by faculty, and one must ask why. Two reasons are dominant, I think. First, the increased focus on student learning holds faculty members accountable for what their students have learned. In the older paradigm, faculty members were judged to be good if they were good teachers, knew their areas well, contributed their share of service to the school, and were engaged in research and writing for the church or academy, or both. Faculty members have direct control of all of these things. The emphasis on student learning is threatening to faculty because they do not have direct control over whether students learn or not. It is one thing to assess student learning and, if a student has failed to learn, the student fails. It is another thing to assess student learning, and if no learning has occurred, the teacher fails. The second reason is that much of the assessment movement has been oriented to quantitative assessment, and theological faculty are rightly concerned that the learning they most want students to attain is not easily measured by these means. I could not agree more with this concern. What I most hope that students learn, what the ATS standards emphasize most — "an aptitude for theological reflection and wisdom pertaining to responsible life in faith" — is not readily evaluated by quantitative strategies. Some quantitative strategies are appropriate for the goals of theological learning and should be used, but there are far more qualitative strategies to assessing this kind of learning that are available.[19]

Assessment of learning is a huge issue, is not going away, and will continue to influence theological schools. As students have become more diverse, as information has become more prolific, as ministry has become more complex, as religion in North America has become more stressed, theological educators need to become more skilled at assessing educational goals for the sake of communities of faith *and* the faith that shapes those communities. Because the work that graduates of theological schools do is important, it is the schools' responsibility to make sure that graduates know all that is necessary to do it well. Theological schools need to become more intentional and skillful about assessing the outcomes of student learning.

In the end, theological schools do not have a choice about developing more intentional and skillful practices of educational assessment. Their choice is to engage assessment of learning grumpily because it has been externally mandated, or to do it faithfully because they care about the subjects they teach, the work of their graduates, and the communities they serve. The assessment of learning for religious vocation is, in the final analysis, an issue of stewardship. Theological schools, like most education in North America, exist for communities beyond themselves and assessment of learning is a primary means by which they exercise accountability to those communities.

---

19. The ATS Commission on Accrediting has been working hard on this issue and has published guidance on assessing learning for religious vocation in its *Handbook of Accreditation*, Section Eight, "A Guide for Evaluating Theological Learning."

Theological Learning and Learning in Ministry

Seminary taught me a great deal. It formed and, in many ways, transformed me. The stories with which this chapter began were not illustrations that I dredged up to introduce the topic. They are part of who I am thirty-five years after these events happened. Seminary did not teach me some lessons that I needed to learn, however. My first year as a pastor exposed me to many of them. I had grown accustomed to the gentle rhythms of academic life, where most of the teachers and students changed every semester, where an occasional bad professor could be waited out and the best professors offered still another course, and where the less good work of a difficult semester did not determine the quality of the work for the next semester. School provided an addictive world of clear time frames, frequent changes, regularized opportunities to start over again, and limited carryover from the previous four months' work to the next four months' work. Pastoral ministry was not like that. People remembered bad sermons, even if they were gracious about them, and difficult parishioners did not leave at the end of the semester. I was not prepared for how emotional a task pastoral ministry can be, how easy it is to do it poorly, and how difficult it is to do it well.

Did seminary somehow fail me in this other kind of learning? Or is there learning that even good schools cannot provide?

School-based theological learning is deeply influenced by the nature of a school — its "school-ness" — for lack of a better term. Schools have particular characteristics and do their work in particular ways, and both of these influence learning. One characteristic of schools is that they are peer-oriented environments. Students are in classes with one another, and there are always more students than professors. While a school has a highly ordered power structure with faculty and administrators on top, students spend most of their time relating to other students. In a school, there are almost always other students to discuss a problem with over a cup of coffee. Another characteristic is that schools gather people in intellectually "safe" spaces, so there is room to explore new ideas and embrace new information. A school is responsible for providing a learning environment that is emotionally open. Schools work hard to remove threats to the intellectual and emotional freedom needed for theological learning. Furthermore, school-based learning is typically highly controlled. A course begins with a syllabus that tells students what they should read, when they should read it, what they should learn from it, and how they should be able to demonstrate their learning. The map is clear, the objectives are stated, and the course is set. The completion of one course is linked to another, under a carefully proscribed curriculum. In this way, a school orders material for students, distinguishes one kind of material from another, provides an organized exposure to it, and sequences that exposure to enhance learning. There are many variables, of course, but the center of "school-ness" education is articulated and focused. Schools divide content into units or disciplines so faculty can gain expertise in an area and the curriculum can be organized according to content. Disciplines provide the internal structure necessary for the school's work to be done well.

Schools, and classroom-based education, are particularly suited for learning that emerges from information in books, teachers, and human interaction. It is very good for the assimilation of material, for relating material in one subject to another. It is ideal for the pursuit of the kind of intellectual work that explores ideas and imagines new combinations and interpretations of those ideas. Schools are superb at facilitating certain kinds of learning. If a person wants to exegete the Greek New Testament, there are few better ways to learn how to do it than to go to a theological school, take an elementary Greek course, then intermediate Greek grammar, and then exegetical courses. If a person wants to learn the history of the church, there are few better ways to do it than to go to a school, take a course on early Christian origins, then a course in early church to the Reformation, then church history post-Reformation to the modern era, and finish with a history of the person's ecclesial community. A school is a wonderful educational strategy. It has shown itself to be durable and effective across cultures and over time.

Schools, with their resources and continuity, can do more than teach Greek and church history. I believe that theological schools are among the best educational strategies available for accomplishing the development of theological understanding. The reason schools are good at this kind of learning is precisely because of the particular characteristics of schools as institutions and the particular way in which they do their work.

The Church of God Theological Seminary asks some students to speak at graduation services, and one year, an international student said, "We don't come here to stay, we came to go." A school is never meant to be a destination. All good theological students, if they complete their course of study, commence from their schools in ceremonies and move into settings that invite a different kind of learning.

Most professional degree graduates of theological schools will move into positions of ministry following graduation, and most of those in ministry will go to congregations. While school is basically a peer-oriented environment, pastoral work, especially for new graduates in smaller congregations, is typically not peer-oriented. Of course, there are peer relationships in the sense that pastor and church members work together out of their baptismal faith. But pastoral leadership requires a unique pattern of engagement in the congregation. The pastor may not be alone in the community of faith, but is alone in terms of role and responsibility to the congregation. If schools gather people into a safe and welcoming space, ministry often throws new graduates into spaces that are as likely to be threatening and unsafe as warm and welcoming. If a school divides work into orderly units, ministry contexts confound work into chaotic and disorganized patterns. If schools are particularly good for the intellectual tasks necessary for the acquisition of material from books, ministry settings are particularly good for intellectual tasks that call for discernment across a wide range of individual and organizational ambiguities. If schools invent disciplines to organize work, ministry contexts have a way of smashing disciplines apart because the categories don't hold up in pastoral practice.

Congregational settings are incredible contexts for learning, but the learning tends to be of a different quality and character. Roger

Shinn, in an essay now many decades old, wrote that ". . . perhaps the most significant education cannot be programmed. There are times of shaking foundations, times of trauma, times of revelation that bring new apprehensions of life and the world. Often they are the very experiences that civilized and compassionate education tries to spare people."[20] Congregational and other ministry settings help graduates learn to think more clinically, administratively, organizationally, and interpersonally. These settings don't teach novice ministers how to "apply" what they learned in school. Rather, these environments evoke different "intelligences." As recent graduates engage in ministry, their dominant intellectual work requires the kind of wisdom that accrues from practices, from skills that get better with repetition and reflection, from perceptions that are informed and enriched by coaching. These lessons are not learned well in a classroom; in fact, they *can't be* learned in a classroom. I remember the first time in ministry when I left the joy of new parents at the hospital delivery room to go to the funeral home. How does one learn to move from celebrating birth to grieving death in two miles? No seminary can teach that in a course. It is learned in the car on the drive between the two, and in the late night, reflecting on the day's events. It is an altogether different kind of learning. Thomas Long, who teaches preaching at Candler School of Theology at Emory University, told a story about a recent seminary graduate who had to do his first funeral that week. The student called his old professor, not sure what he needed to do. The professor reminded the student of what had been covered in the worship and preaching class, including funerals. Interrupting the professor, the student anxiously replied, "But this guy is really *dead!*"[21] Crushing life and death issues are everyday occurrences in parish and congregational life, and they are powerful teachers to an attentive pastor.

Pastoral work is a constant variation around certain themes. Like jazz, pastoral work is improvisational, and improvisation requires

20. Roger Shinn, "Education Is a Mystery," in *A Colloquy on Christian Education*, ed. John H. Westerhoff III (Philadelphia: United Church Press, 1972), p. 19.

21. Thomas Long's project as a Henry Luce III Fellow in Theology during 1995-1996 was "The Christian Funeral in American Context."

knowing both the tune and how to play variations on it.[22] Some recent seminary graduates have been involved in church their whole lives, but others have not. The latter group can graduate without the church equivalent of "street smarts." Their theological schools have done what schools do, focused on more denotative ways of knowing, but the students do not have the education that ministry contexts provide. They need "church smarts," and schools — even very good ones — are not very effective at teaching that kind of "smart." It takes a context of practice and engagement for this kind of knowing.

Having read this far, you know that I am deeply committed to the importance of theological schools for ministerial and priestly education. What does it mean that I end the chapter by saying that there are vital lessons for ministry that schools can't teach? I think schools are invaluable for the education they provide, but that does not mean that they can stimulate all the learning that religious leaders in North America need. *The case for theological schools is not that they can do everything that needs to be done, but that they do many things that are absolutely essential to learning for religious vocation, and they do them better than any other kind of educational program.* Schools are an efficient and effective strategy for the complex and sophisticated learning that good ministry requires, but other, equally complex and important learning depends on other settings and contexts. The case for theological schools recognizes that good ministry requires more than one kind of learning, and different kinds of learning require different educational settings. This is true of medical education, which includes hospital-based training while in medical school and internship and residency training afterward. It is true for legal education, which includes clerkships in addition to law school. It is also true for ministry. Education for ministry requires an educational ecology with varied types of learning and settings.

22. Max De Pree, long-time trustee at Fuller Theological Seminary and chair emeritus of the Herman Miller Company, wrote a book a number of years ago called *Leadership Jazz* (New York: Dell Publishing, 1992) in which he argues that good leadership has a jazz-like, improvisational quality. I think the image is especially useful for understanding pastoral practice.

Schools are crucial for the formational learning that helps faith grow by finding the reasons that give it ballast, that makes knowledge grow in ways that lead to theological wisdom, and that helps learners through the difficult religious terrain of moving from uninformed to informed belief. Theological learning is at the heart of the work of theological schools.

CHAPTER 3

Teaching and Research
in Theological Schools

David Scholer is a professor at Fuller Theological Seminary. He has been teaching and researching the New Testament for decades and, in 2007, was the subject of an article in the *Los Angeles Times*. At age 68, he is now teaching with incurable cancer. He told the reporter that for much of his career, he had "puzzled over a line from 1 Thessalonians: 'Rejoice always, pray continually, give thanks in all circumstances; for this is God's will for you in Christ Jesus.'" He asked, "How did one 'give thanks in all circumstances'? In tragedy? Sickness?" These days, he lectures sitting down, uses a cane when he walks, and tells students about his disease at the beginning of each course, primarily to explain his physical condition and potential absences. While his physical capacity has weakened, his pedagogical capacity has strengthened. Students who have been in his classes these past few years have learned their lessons. "Clarissa Chng, a former student, remembers what he said on her first day in his class: Seminarians are called to a higher standard and greater responsibility. 'You have burned the bridges of naiveté, and there is no more turning back.' Chng said she often reflects on Scholer's words. 'Every time I am faced with a difficult decision and find myself wishing that I could take the easy way out by feigning ignorance, I remember his words and realize that I must take responsibility for the knowledge I have and use it to inform my decision-making, even if that means going through a period of discomfort.'"[1]

Teaching the lessons that form human lives involves discomfort, and when that discomfort is tended properly, it leads to wholeness and integrity. Learning, serious learning about faith and life, requires burning bridges, and theological faculty, at least the best of them, force students to light fires to false assumptions and inadequate understanding, and stand by them as they struggle with life on the knowing side of the charred bridge. David Scholer, like thousands of other faculty members in theological schools in North America, is a teacher.

Teaching, learning, and research are deeply, if not inseparably, related. Twice over the past several years, ATS has convened groups of senior theological scholars to discuss needed research in theological studies and, on both occasions, a surprising amount of the conversation focused on teaching, learning, and curriculum. In a meeting about research, faculty members could not talk about research without talking about the theological curriculum and the nature of theological learning. In another meeting, faculty were asked to address curricular issues and ended up talking about the character of theological learning and their work of teaching. Teaching and learning simply do not exist independently of one another. If there is no learning and no teaching, there is no school. If there is no research, there is nothing new to learn and limited assurance that what was taken for granted in the past is reliable or true.

Teaching

Teaching is an act of scholarship, and at its best, it is as attentive to students as it is to subjects. Teaching that guides students toward theological understanding involves curricular and course design, but it transcends them as well. It is the work of persons who know an area of

---

1. K. Connie Kang, "Rejoice Always: A Lesson in Dying," *Los Angeles Times*, 5 June 2007, www.latimes.com/news/local/la-me-scholer5jun05,0,1943101.story?coll=la-home-center.

theological inquiry intimately well, care about it deeply, understand and value the work for which students are preparing, and engage their students with honesty and integrity. These characteristics have pedagogical power, especially in theological schools, where teaching touches on struggles about ultimate meaning and encounters with intense human commitments.

Strategies and the Educational Aims of Theological Teaching

What strategies and insights does theological teaching require? Susan Simonaitis teaches theology at Fordham University, and in the process of writing an essay on "Teaching as Conversation," asked her students to reflect on teaching. She quotes one freshman's response to her request. "It is not enough for teachers to be brilliant scholars. Nor is it enough for teachers to be entertaining circus side shows. Teachers must be brilliant, passionate, intense, insistent, compelling, and relentless."[2] If this freshman's assessment is true, and I think it is, then teaching is not for the fainthearted. It is complex and demanding work. It can't be done by a talking head; it can only be done by a reflective life. Lois Malcolm, in an essay about teaching in a denominational seminary, argues that seminaries are responsible for educating students for a different world than the one for which they educated students in the past. "At issue in this new context may not be the task of defending Christianity's cognitive claims as much as learning how to use spiritual power appropriately." This is a complicated task for any teacher, and subject to potential misuse, even abuse. So, she goes on to say that this task ". . . entails discerning God's justice and mercy in the full complexity of life, and to do that we cannot escape the difficult task of integrating the multiple dimensions of our lives."[3] Teaching is an act of

2. Susan M. Simonaitis, "Teaching as Conversation," in *The Scope of Our Art: The Vocation of the Theological Teacher,* ed. L. Gregory Jones and Stephanie Paulsell (Grand Rapids: William B. Eerdmans Publishing Co., 2002), p. 100.

3. Lois Malcolm, "Teaching as Cultivating Wisdom for a Complex World," in *The Scope of Our Art,* p. 154.

scholarship that is intellectual, relational, and personal. Good teaching is equally attentive to students and subjects.

The work of the theological teacher is nowhere described better or documented more thoughtfully than in the report of a project by The Carnegie Foundation for the Advancement of Teaching. Carnegie has conducted a decade-long study on education for the professions. The "Preparation for the Professions Program" has completed studies of the education of engineers, lawyers, and clergy at the time of this writing. Research on nurse and physician education is currently under way. The Carnegie study of clergy education[4] researched a wide range of Christian and Jewish seminaries. It included extensive interviews with faculty and students, observation of classes in each of the subject schools, surveys of faculty completed in conjunction with research at the Auburn Center for the Study of Theological Education, reading many of the books written by professors whose classes were visited, and comparison of findings from theological schools with the findings from research in other professional schools.

Charles Foster and his collaborators on this project found that teaching in theological schools tended to focus on four areas: interpretation, formation, contextualization, and performance. Together, they concluded that these four pedagogical intentions constituted what Lee Schulman, president of The Carnegie Foundation for the Advancement of Teaching, has called a "signature pedagogy." A signature pedagogy is a "window" into "what counts most significantly as the essence of a profession's work." For example, the signature pedagogy in medicine, with its focus on diagnosis and treatment, is the professor and students "centered on an individual patient in a hospital bed."[5] No other form of professional education has this unique pedagogical practice. If you wanted a picture of medical education, what could be better than one of a professor in a lab coat standing by a patient's bedside, chart in hand, young students in lab coats listening carefully?

4. Charles R. Foster, Lisa E. Dahill, Lawrence A. Goleman, and Barbara Wang Tolentino, *Educating Clergy: Teaching Practices and Pastoral Imagination* (San Francisco: Jossey-Bass, 2006).

5. Foster et al., *Educating Clergy,* pp. 32-33.

This picture would hardly need a caption. What would be a picture of the signature pedagogy for theological education? According to the Carnegie researchers, there is none. The signature pedagogy in theological education is discernibly present but not readily visible. It is the faculty as a whole, course after course, in different ways, in different combinations, teaching students with a focus on interpretation, contextualization, performance, and formation. Students don't experience one of these pedagogical strategies in biblical studies and another in pastoral care or preaching. They experience many of them, in different combinations, in most of the classes they have.

Theological faculty members spend a great deal of time on the *interpretation* of texts. Most theological learning is textually based, and interpretation is crucial to theological learning and pastoral practice. Interpretation is a complex activity. The researchers observed how professor Cheryl Sanders, who teaches social ethics at Howard University School of Divinity, taught students to interpret texts. The process she uses, and the one she wants students to learn, involves "capacities for *reading* and *analyzing* texts, situations, and relationships."[6] Interpretation is never only about a text; it is a process of using a text in the context of situations and relationships. These characteristics of interpretation are closely associated with how theological educators understand critical thinking.

Formational pedagogy aims at students learning "dispositions, habits, knowledge, and skills that cohere in professional identity and practice, commitments and integrity."[7] Formational learning is critical to theological studies, and it is central to the deepest intentions in professional service that are present in medicine, law, and teaching. Wendy Rosov, who conducted an ethnographic study of a Jewish seminary, writes about a professor of philosophy and administrator who has a plaque in Hebrew that translates, "I set the Lord always before me." The professor told Rosov, "It means that wherever you are and whatever you are doing, that's a chance to encounter God and be with

6. Foster et al., *Educating Clergy*, p. 89.
7. Foster et al., *Educating Clergy*, p. 100.

65

God. . . . I'd like to find a way to cultivate that in my students."[8] This commitment is about a habit, a disposition that this professor wants his students to learn, and almost every faculty member in an ATS school can identify habits, dispositions, or skills that they want to cultivate in their students. This is formational teaching. Students who have learned the practice of the presence of God, who have learned to attend to the mystery that is the first and last chapter of true religion, have been formed for ministry.

The third pedagogy, *contextualization,* is the "task of making explicit the socially situated nature of all knowledge and practice." To function faithfully in ministry, students need to learn the contexts of texts, historical events, religious practices, and ministerial work. Contexts are not just backgrounds that serve as settings for texts or religious practices. "Contexts consist of patterns of relationship and social structures, historical trajectories and local particularities, status and power configurations, values and commitments, and dispositions and habits. . . ."[9] The researchers illustrate this pedagogy from their visit to Thomas Narin's class in medical ethics at Catholic Theological Union. Narin uses case studies in his course, and he wants students to learn first by reacting to the facts of a case, then retrieving the Catholic tradition as it might relate to them, a process he calls critical correlation. He then guides students in reconstructing an ethical analysis. Medical technology changes so rapidly that it is not possible to come to an ethical conclusion that lasts a long time. Students have to learn a process that they can use to derive an ethical judgment as both the facts and medical science change. The process is contextualization, and it relates to many activities in theological study and ministry practice. It is a way to bring religion's long and ancient traditions in dialogue with current realities, and it is a crucial form of theological learning.

A final pedagogical focus is on *performance.* Ministry is a public profession, and students need to learn the performance skills that

---

8. Quoted in Foster et al., *Educating Clergy,* p. 108.
9. Foster et al., *Educating Clergy,* pp. 132, 129.

preaching, liturgy, public leadership, and other ministerial tasks require. Developing competence in the performance of the public dimensions of ministry is crucial to the leadership of communities of faith; it is not performance for its own sake. The minister or priest "performs" as a person of faith, and this performance guides the community into its own shared and corporate faith. When the minister reads the leader's line in responsive liturgy, it is a "performance." But the line is read to guide the congregation in reading its line. The purpose of this liturgical "performance" is not just to introduce some variation in the service by reading responsively; it is to declare and reinforce the shared belief of the community. The result of good performance is not applause, it is a community reminded of its faith and, hopefully, strengthened in it. Ministerial performance does not entail an actor taking on a character. Rather, it is an outward, public representation of an inward disposition. The process of learning "to perform" should strengthen students' faith, just as participating in the "performance" in worship should strengthen the faith of worshipers. The researchers note that "engaging students through pedagogies of performance includes paying attention to the importance of their spiritual and vocational formation."[10]

Faculty and Teaching

Several years ago, three colleagues and I were involved in an ethnographic study of two theological schools. Over the course of three years, we made frequent visits to the schools, sat in on classes, interviewed faculty, spent nights in student housing, visited churches where students were doing their fieldwork, attended study groups, went to chapel, read the campus bulletin boards, and, in other appropriate ways, participated in campus life. In the last semester of the third year, my colleague conducted individual interviews with all of the students with whom we had worked closely, and together we had conversations with most of these students in group meetings. We asked

10. Foster et al., *Educating Clergy*, p. 181.

how they had changed across these three years and what had influenced them most. We asked how the faculty impacted them as well. In three years, we had sat in classes taught by every faculty member at the seminary, usually in more than one course, and had conducted lengthy interviews with each professor. We had our ideas about the most influential faculty, and our suspicions about the least effective. To our surprise, every faculty member at the school was identified as an important influence by at least one student. The professors that we thought were the most influential had impacted the largest number of students, but even the faculty members we suspected had influenced no one had touched someone in meaningful ways. Our hunches about the faculty were only partly right. Every one of them had deeply influenced at least some students. Some were better teachers than others, some were more popular, some were more persuasive lecturers, but these variables did not predict which faculty members would have the greatest impact on any one student. Maybe that freshman in Professor Simonaitis's class was right. "Teachers must be brilliant, passionate, intense, insistent, compelling, and relentless." In different ways and to different degrees, the faculty we observed for three years all exhibited this demanding list of qualities.

The 2003 survey of faculty in ATS schools conducted by the Auburn Center for the Study of Theological Education found that, "Faculty 'strongly agree' that teaching for them has a spiritual or religious character, and they are almost as likely to agree with the statement that they 'rely on God's presence while teaching.' "[11] Teaching has a significant impact on students. More than half of the ATS member schools participate in the ATS *Graduating Student Questionnaire,* and while responses to some questions vary, graduating students respond to one question almost exactly the same, year after year. When asked to identify the most influential aspect of their theological education, among fifteen choices, the first choice is always the faculty. Other aspects of theological education are influential, but "faculty" tops the

---

11. Barbara G. Wheeler, Sharon L. Miller, and Katarina Schuth, "Signs of the Times," *Auburn Studies,* no. 10 (February 2005): 21.

list and, year after year, it is named by twice the percentage of students as the second most frequently chosen influence. Learning is the first job of theological schools, and teachers, more than anything else, make learning possible.

Theological Research

As part of its Henry Luce III Fellows in Theology program, the Association sponsored a major consultation on theological research in 2003.[12] It involved almost one hundred scholars from theological schools across North America who worked through a series of small group discussions about the nature of theological scholarship, research that should be addressed, and the agenda for future research in the theological disciplines. The summary of one of the thirty group sessions included a lament that "people should stop writing so much!" When the comment was included in the end-of-conference report session, everyone chuckled. Participants in this conference valued research, wrote a great deal, and read even more, but they also identified with the remark. Some senior scholars at that meeting could remember a time, early in their careers, when they could read most of the literature in their focused area of study. Now, the literature is too voluminous for any one person to read, even in highly specialized areas. The exponential growth of new information begets more and more writing about narrower and narrower areas of inquiry. Beneath the chuckle, I think there was a sobering intellectual concern. Current academic expectations seem to value the production of research regarding very specific areas of knowledge more highly than critical contemplation of larger intellectual issues.

---

12. The summary report of the consultation was published as "ATS Luce Consultation on Theological Scholarship, May 2003" in *Theological Education* 40, no. 2 (2005): 93-114.

Criticisms of Academic Theological Research

This lament, if it were that, was embedded in the discussion of thoughtful theological educators who have been productive researchers and writers. They were not anti-research in their attitudes and, in fact, spent most of the consultation talking about the kind of research that was most needed. These participants wanted research that focused in different directions or reflected more crucial topics. This group reflected the same concerns that the ATS Council on Theological Scholarship and Research expressed a decade earlier. At the conclusion of its work, the Council wrote that without research, "neither teaching nor the derivative learning dependent on it could either exist at all or ever be improved."[13]

Two divergent critiques have been leveled against theological research. The first is that theological research is often irrelevant. The irrelevance criticism likely emerges from the pragmatic and practical tendencies in American thought: why conduct a research project if there is no clear implication or application? Technical theological research can seem very removed from the struggle and angst of contemporary Christian engagement — like some modern-day version of that medieval question (for which there is no scholarly evidence that it was ever asked): "How many angels can dance on the head of a pin?" The second critique is almost the opposite; it worries that the research is not sufficiently scholarly or objective. As academic research in religion developed in the last half of the twentieth century, an increasing division emerged between theological studies and religious studies. The divide is more polemical than real, but as American church historian Mark Toulouse notes, one small academic society for the study of religion "has made clear its argument that religious studies departments should not include theologians because they believe in God." Toulouse quotes a founder of the society: "There's the academic study of religion, and there's the religious study of religion." The perception here

13. Open letter to ATS member schools, the Council on Theological Scholarship and Research, 1992.

is that, "The former is scholarly and critical; the other is not."[14] Some scholars of religion think that theological research is inherently anti-intellectual because the researchers engage their work from a perspective of faith and often direct their efforts to both church and academic audiences.

The first of these critiques has a point. Some research, even to serious scholarly analysts, is, like Shakespeare's play: much ado about nothing! Some research topics can be highly idiosyncratic and unworthy of the effort they require. However, theological research does not have to have an immediate usefulness in order to be valuable. Concluding that research is irrelevant because the topic is silly is different from concluding that research is irrelevant because it has no immediate, pragmatic usefulness. The second critique is objectionable in all cases. Believing does not cripple a person intellectually, and the presumption that one can pursue truth better apart from belief is itself a belief.

Research is crucial to the vitality of the Christian project; research can be both intellectually rigorous and faithful; research can be important even without immediate implications. A careful comparison of a good contemporary English translation of the Bible to older translations will demonstrate the contributions that the past century of research on ancient languages and manuscripts has made for a more faithful reading of sacred text. Much of the research that resulted in this more intellectually robust translation was highly technical and must have seemed incredibly irrelevant at the time. Current theological research in North America reflects far more of the cultural, ethnic, and racial reality that characterizes worldwide Christianity than was true fifty years ago. These are important changes that will help both communities of faith and theological scholars, as North American Christianity becomes increasingly multicultural and finds the wisdom from the entire community of faith, not just one part of it.

14. Mark G. Toulouse, "Crafting Research that Will Contribute to Theological Education," *Theological Education* 40, no. 2 (2005): 117.

Theological Research that "Matters"

The most obvious way to overcome the criticisms that research sometimes attracts is to engage in research that matters. Making the determination of what matters is more difficult in theological research than in
science or technology. The outcomes of theological research never result
in "breakthrough" discoveries like those scientific researchers sometimes achieve. The "new" findings of theological research seldom replace existing perceptions: they are more likely to modify them. A new
understanding of sin or salvation must be in dialogue with understandings about sin and salvation from the fourth century, the Reformation,
and last century. Theological research accumulates over centuries and
broadens over continents. North American research about judgment or
grace is not sufficiently scholarly if it fails to engage the perspectives on
judgment and grace of Asian or African or Latin American theological
thinkers. In theological research, "new" understandings are never defin-
itive or final. Theological research begins and ends with the inability to
know fully what it most wants to know, like understanding God truly.[15]
Because theological research is ultimately about the ineffable, it requires
scholars to go about their work with a deep and pervasive humility.

ATS faculty are active researchers. It is not all they do; most say
they are primarily teachers. But the majority of faculty members conduct research and publish their findings. In the early 1990s, the Auburn
Center for the Study of Theological Education studied the publication
rates of the ATS faculty. About one-third of ATS faculty members did
no scholarly publishing, although most of this group wrote for church
audiences. The other two-thirds tended to write both for the scholarly
community and for more general readers. Tenured faculty members
publish at a higher rate than nontenured faculty, and the younger half
of tenured faculty publish at the highest rate of any group.[16] In a sec-

---

15. "Knowing God truly" is David Kelsey's phrase for the ultimate goal of theological education. *To Understand God Truly: What's Theological About a Theological School* (Louisville, Ky.: Westminster/John Knox Press, 1992).

16. Barbara G. Wheeler, "True and False," *Auburn Studies*, no. 4 (January 1996):
16.

ond survey a decade later, the Auburn researchers asked faculty if they emphasized teaching or research more. Only one percent of faculty said that research was their primary focus, compared with 29 percent who said that their primary focus was teaching. The other 70 percent of ATS faculty focused on some combination of both: 34 percent "lean toward teaching," 24 percent weight teaching and research equally, and 13 percent "lean toward research."[17]

What are the qualities of good theological research? This question can be answered in many ways, but I will suggest two. Good research, first of all, must be methodologically sound. A primary role of academic guilds is to establish technical criteria for good research methods. The Society of Biblical Literature, for example, provides the best venue for identifying the technically correct ways to conduct research in biblical languages and ancient manuscripts. The Society for the Scientific Study of Religion provides the best venue for scholars to identify appropriate research practices in the sociological and social psychological study of religion. Good research, secondly, must also address issues of substance, subjects that really matter. While the methodological criteria for good research can be left to the guilds, it does not follow that the agenda of research itself — what subjects are the most important to study at a particular time — should also be left to them. The agenda of research has a wider community of accountability than the methodology of research, and determining what should be studied requires different criteria than determining good methodology.

Who determines the criteria that identify which research subjects should be studied? That is a question for which every interested party likely has a different answer. For more than a decade, the Association has sponsored two major programs that together have provided more than a half million dollars annually in support of theological research projects. Between one and two hundred applicants submit proposals each year to these programs. I do not have a vote on the selection committees, but I read the proposals, listen to the committee's delibera-

---

17. Wheeler et al., "Signs of the Times," p. 20.

tions, and sometimes enter the conversation. All in all, I have read well over a thousand faculty proposals in the past decade, and that experience has taught me that I don't know which of many good projects should be funded! A few proposals have not been good, and in these competitions they are relatively easy to spot. However, it is far more difficult to determine which of many excellent proposals should be funded. Each research grants program has selection criteria, but most of the proposals meet them. When the committee has more than five times the number of proposals than can be funded, all of which meet the criteria of the program, what other criteria contribute to the decisions? As I listen to committees' discussions, the issue of "what matters" seems central to their deliberations. I'd like to propose several criteria for theological research that matters and illustrate them by projects these selection committees have funded over the years. I need to make clear, however, that these are my personal views, not the criteria of programs sponsored by ATS or, in the final analysis, the criteria employed by the selection committees.

Research that matters addresses particular intellectual agendas or needs in ecclesial communities. Of all the differences associated with theological schools, none is more influential than the ecclesial family to which the school is related: Evangelical Protestant, mainline Protestant, and Roman Catholic or Orthodox. Many pressing intellectual questions differ by these communities. A proposal on a postcolonial reinterpretation of Pauline approaches to legal texts is more likely to come from a mainline Protestant scholar than an Evangelical one; a proposal on *nouvelle théologie* is more likely to come from a Roman Catholic scholar than a mainline Protestant one; and a proposal on openness theology is more likely to come from a particular kind of Evangelical scholar than a Roman Catholic one. While the intellectual discourse across communities shares many common elements, discourse within one community often varies a great deal from the discourse in another community. Research matters when it addresses the particular problems and questions of particular communities. Each community needs good intellectual effort, which requires researchers to know the questions and proclivities of the community they most want to address. "Good" research topics are not determined by making the intellectual questions of any one ecclesial community the premiere questions for the intellectual work of all of them.

Kenneth Keathley was engaged in a project a few years ago on "Salvation and the Sovereignty of God."[18] For many theological researchers, that might sound like a rather ordinary topic, researched over centuries now, and not on the edge of new scholarship. Keathley, however, teaches at a seminary funded by the Southern Baptist Convention (SBC), and at the time he worked on this project, the SBC was struggling with this very issue. Southern Baptist thinking reflects an amalgamation of Reformed and Arminian leanings, and this unique combination has emerged as an issue as the SBC is renegotiating its current theological understandings. Keathley's research sought to identify resolutions to this tension that are faithful to the denomination's theological traditions. At about the same time, Samuel Elolia was working on a project about "the Holy Spirit and the African Indigenous Churches." The tension between missionary expressions of Christianity and indigenous African expressions is a serious contest in present-day African Christianity. This is not an issue in North America, but Christianity is not a North American possession, and the contests in Africa will influence the life of a globalized church. Elolia, as an African national working in a U.S. seminary, may be able to make a needed scholarly contribution[19] to an issue that is almost too hot to handle in parts of Africa. Theological research matters to the extent that it addresses intellectual issues important to particular communities in particular contexts; after all, the particular is the most universal characteristic of religion.

Theological research that matters serves the broader purposes of religion. Religion deals with life and death. It deals with meanings

18. Kenneth D. Keathley, "Salvation and the Sovereignty of God: Exploring the Incarnational Approach" (Lilly Theological Research Grants research project, New Orleans Baptist Theological Seminary, 2005-06).

19. Samuel K. Elolia, "African Pneumatology: The Holy Spirit and the African Indigenous Churches" (Lilly Theological Research Grants research project, Emmanuel School of Religion, 2005-06).

that shape lives, enable human beings to cope with unbearable trauma, and order their vision of the world. Finding a way for people of different world religions to make peace together is not an expression of politically correct multiculturalism; it may be the most crucial new skill for humans to develop in this century. Religion can give life, and it can kill. Research should understand that religion is about life-ordering issues and death-defining moments. Research that serves religion does not make a point of its self-importance, but it knows, beneath the footnotes, that it is dealing with the core of human longing and hoping. Theological research matters most when the researcher understands the deep purposes of the Christian faith. Robert A. Krieg had this in mind when he undertook a study of Catholic theologians in Nazi Germany. How does the church deal with political power when it turns evil? Jon Levenson explored the big issues that religion addresses in his study of Christian and Jewish images of life after death.[20] No one theological research project settles these large issues. They are, in the end, irresolvable, which is exactly why researchers should return to them as cultural assumptions and understandings change.

Research that matters sometimes deals with issues that are very deep in the scholarly infrastructure. Frank Gruber became president of Chicago Lutheran Seminary in 1928, and in his inaugural address, he bemoaned the fragmentation and overspecialization that he thought was rampant in theological education early in the twentieth century. To demonstrate how bad it really was, he quoted the deathbed lament of a famed, but unnamed, German professor. "If I had to do it all over again . . . I would devote my entire life to the study of the iota subscript." (The iota subscript is a marking under certain vowels in Greek.) Ralph Klein used Gruber's quote in the editorial introduction to an issue of a journal and wrote: "Seminary education attempts to

20. Robert A. Krieg, "Catholic Theologians in Hitler's Germany" (Luce Fellows in Theology research project, University of Notre Dame Department of Theology, 2001-2002) and Jon D. Levenson, "The Tree of Life: The Loss, Recovery, and Redefinition of Immortality in Judaism and Christianity" (Luce Fellows in Theology research project, Harvard University Divinity School, 1999-2000).

prepare church leaders who are able to witness to the reconciling Word of God, both through their lives and ministries. . . . The scholarship that supports these lofty goals is often detailed, abstract, nonutilitarian and difficult, though not necessarily lost in the wonders of the iota subscript."[21] Someone needs to devote a life to the iota subscript. Gay Byron has studied manuscripts from early Christian churches in what is now Ethiopia. The language is quite remote, survives only in some liturgy of the Ethiopian Orthodox Church, and, as a result, these manuscripts remain largely unknown in the West. Her work will not make a difference in any sermon next year, but it will be noticed by other scholars, who will use her analysis of these ancient texts to amplify their interpretations of more familiar texts, which will be used in the writing of future commentaries that will be read by pastors and, several links along a chain of learning, will influence a Sunday sermon or a Wednesday pastor's class.[22]

Research that matters speaks to important human conditions. Nancy Eiesland has worked on theological research related to persons with disabilities. Bonnie Miller-McLemore has worked on research related to the theology and care of children in Western culture. Meanwhile, Emilie Townes has been researching how culture builds and sustains racist images that perpetuate the unethical categorization of racial groups.[23] This research brings the wisdom of the Christian tradition and its compelling moral voice to issues that need both. It is research that matters.

21. *Currents in Theology and Mission* (April 2000): 82.
22. Gay L. Byron, "Utilizing the Legacy of Ancient Ethiopians and Ethiopia for the Study of the New Testament and Christian Origins" (Luce Fellows in Theology research project, Colgate Rochester Crozier Divinity School, 2005-06).
23. Nancy Eiesland, "Reverence and the Complex Human Condition: Theological Reflections on Living Disability" (Lilly Theological Scholars Grants research project, Candler School of Theology of Emory University, 2005-06); Bonnie Miller-McLemore, "Toward a Theology of Children: Care of Children as a Religious Discipline and Communal Practice" (Luce Fellows in Theology research project, Vanderbilt University Divinity School, 1999-2000); and Emilie M. Townes, "Sites of Memory: Dismantling the Cultural Production of Evil" (Luce Fellows in Theology research project, Yale University Divinity School, 2005-06).

Research that matters can also address wrongheaded tendencies in religious practice. John Stackhouse is exploring a theology of culture that would provide a way around two tendencies with which some North American Evangelical Christians are currently infatuated: a holy withdrawal from the world, on the one hand, or re-making the world into a very particular Christian pattern, on the other. Stackhouse wants to explore an alternative that is "more ambiguous, more ambivalent, dialectical, realistic, and tense" than these models. Perhaps only an academic researcher would want more ambiguity, ambivalence, and dialecticism, but these may be exactly the qualities that faithful religion may need to counter the tendency that wants easy, categorical answers to issues that are nuanced and complex.[24]

There are, no doubt, other criteria that could be used to identify the kind of theological research that matters. It would surprise me if persons who are most engaged in theological research would come up with the same list, but for me, research that addresses the needs of particular communities, that serves broad religious purposes and discussions, that informs the infrastructure of theological research, that addresses the human condition, and that seeks to reform misguided religious practices is research that matters. No one project can meet all of these criteria, but the research enterprise, as a whole, can.

Threats to Research

Research that matters, of course, is not enough. Even if the criteria that I have identified are met and the methodology is sound, research can still be threatened.

One threat is that communities of faith too often ignore or resist thoughtful findings. Most research is valuable but not controversial, and that research is sometimes ignored. If good research is completed that relates to a particular community's needs, it does little good, in

24. John G. Stackhouse, "Cultivating the Garden, Building the City: A Theology of Cultural Persistence" (Lilly Faculty Fellowship research project, Regent College, 2005-06).

the end, if the community will not pay attention to it. The anti-intellectual leanings in some expressions of North American religion fuel a perception that academic theology is sufficiently irrelevant that nothing researchers find can be of much value. There is also, at times, an unwillingness to work hard on issues. Various streams of North American religion reach out in the culture by requiring little effort on the part of adherents. The spiritual discipline of study is celebrated by some but ignored by many. I have sat in meetings with good theological researchers, who care a great deal about the church and the faith, who have something to say that needs to be heard, and listened as they expressed frustrations on this issue. Important contributions can die for lack of reading and study.

Every once in a while, research generates controversial findings and the history of the Christian church is replete with examples of those findings being rejected, sometimes along with the researcher. Different ecclesial communities of faith have different centers of teaching authority. However, any ecclesial body needs the capacity to listen to findings that challenge the status quo but can renew and strengthen theological understanding. Not all new ideas are better or more faithful, but churches need to be able to hear them and test the academic spirits. Sometimes, the new idea is a work of the Spirit, not just the researcher. At the 2003 Luce Conference on Theological Scholarship, some scholars jokingly referred to the difference between research in secular universities and research in their theological schools. In the former, it is "publish or perish;" in the latter, it is "publish *and* perish." Theological schools and church bodies have the right to order doctrinal commitments and hold persons who work in their structures accountable to that ordering. However, communities of faith that are incapable of hearing challenges to cherished ideas or altogether new perceptions of faith threaten the integrity of their faith. The faith that has been once for all delivered to the saints has not necessarily been understood, once for all. The church that was built on the Rock can become a rock. While rocks are sturdy, good for foundations, they have no life, and cannot become "living stones" that form communities of living faith.

The second threat is difficulty inherent in communicating research written in technical language to nonscholarly audiences. At one time, theological scholars could write in technical, scholarly language, and agencies within then-robust denominational structures translated this scholarly research into essays and other resources that were readily used by lay audiences. Many of those denominational structures are weaker now and no longer have the capacity to generate the translated, popularized literature. Many scholars today must be able to write both technically, so that other scholars can evaluate and use their work, and popularly, so the research is accessible to a wider audience. This reality makes the difficult work of research more complicated, even threatens it. Fortunately, some of the best theological scholars have developed the ability to write both narrowly and technically and broadly and appealingly.

A third threat to research that matters is the research agenda. If researchers don't address issues that matter, if they expend their intellectual talent on arcane issues of limited value by any criteria for theological research, then both the academy and the church lose a needed resource. Not all subjects matter, however interesting they may be to a particular researcher, and part of the art of research is the ability to identify subjects worthy of study. The problem with agenda is not limited to individual choices. Sometimes, scholarly guilds exercise a huge influence on the research agenda, and while the topics they encourage pursuing may be of interest to a few people in the guild, they are far removed from anything crucial to the church's intellectual work. On the one hand, schools and the church should give wide latitude to researchers to work on projects that seem esoteric to nonresearchers. Work needs to be done on infrastructure issues; the criterion for good research is not that it is immediately useful or applicable. On the other hand, researchers have a responsibility to pursue projects that serve a broader function than idiosyncratic, individual interests. There have been times when the church has experienced great trauma or profound change — the very events that could benefit from thoughtful theological research — and researchers busied themselves with work that ignored them.

Theological research is not always well understood outside of the school, and that lack of understanding is evident in discussions about sabbatical leaves. Most ATS faculty have a work week that is full of teaching classes, meeting with students, working in seminary committees, providing service to churches and denominations, and reading to stay current in their fields. If they are to engage in serious research, most faculty members need time apart from their weekly duties, and that has traditionally taken the form of a research or sabbatical leave. People outside higher education often see these leaves as either costly luxuries or irrelevant holdovers from the past — corporate executives and business owners certainly don't get them. But research requires focused time on task. A sabbatical leave in an earlier era may have meant time away from regular work for gentlemen scholars to think and reflect — with limited expectations for research. This is increasingly not the case. Research leaves in the modern seminary provide time to engage in focused work that cannot be done among all the other routine activities of seminary life. Leaves provide time to read in depth, renew one's own thinking, and contribute to the thinking of others. It is not vacation or time away from work; it is time on a different task, at a different pace, that is deeply a part of a theological school's work, which cannot be accomplished in the typically busy days of seminary faculty.

Another misunderstood aspect of academic research, and sometimes teaching, is the practice of tenure. Critics perceive that tenure protects the unproductive scholar who, in any other employment setting, would be pressured to produce or leave. Occasionally, tenure does protect the unproductive professor and costs the school precious resources. Typically, however, tenure functions as an academic practice that recognizes the value of the unpopular notion and creates an employment environment where faculty members enjoy some protections as they seek truth in their area of expertise. Tenure does not always protect a faculty member, in either secular or theological schools, but it does impose a discipline on the process for removing a professor.

As I observe theological schools, tenure does not appear to be the problem that people fear it is. As noted earlier, Auburn Center data indicate that tenured faculty members publish at the highest rates of any faculty in ATS schools. The bigger problem for schools may be the changes in employment law in both the United States and Canada that have removed the ability of an institution to establish mandatory retirement ages. Theological schools do have problems when a faculty member ceases to be productive but refuses to retire. It is difficult to demonstrate that a faculty member is not performing well in his or her job, at least in the ways that subsequent litigation would require, and most theological schools cannot provide the financial incentives that many corporations do to encourage retirement. A theological faculty needs to renew itself, and, historically, this has happened as faculty members retired at predictable times. However, it's also true that many faculty are capable of some of their best contributions when they are older than previous mandatory retirement ages.

Tenure does pose a risk in theological schools in that it may provide safe haven to a noncontributing faculty member. However, the lack of tenure also poses a risk, if the church values the need to be challenged to rethink and renew its commitments, and this may be the biggest "if" in this essay. The risk of the church *not* having the critical challenge that can renew its thinking is more serious than the risk of an occasional nonproductive faculty member. Tenure provides the disciplined protections that allow theological teachers to pursue important but controversial issues.

Theological research contributes to lively teaching and engaged learning. Students are energized by good faculty research and gain a perspective about its value that they will take with them to positions of religious leadership. Good research serves particular needs in particular communities of faith, takes on big issues in religious belief, does the technical infrastructure work, and brings Christian perspective to particular human needs. It is of great potential value to the church and its understanding of its work and mission. Research is the risk capital of theological education. It requires long-term investment, results are often removed from the effort of the initial research, and applicability is often not immediately apparent. Risk capital finances new ventures and new ideas. Some will fail. Some will succeed. A few will succeed spectacularly. No one knows when the venture starts which of these results will be the outcome. Research is exactly like that. It is the means by which new and fresh theological insights can and often do emerge.

Library as Teacher and Researcher

The Wesley Theological Seminary campus was designed with the chapel and library juxtaposed, with glass walls on their facing sides. Study and worship are architecturally connected at Wesley, and on the corner of the library is a stone inscribed with a famous John Wesley quotation: "Unite the pair so long disjoined, knowledge and vital piety." The library at St. John's University in Minnesota has structural columns that expand in tree-like branches, reminding knowledge seekers of the Garden's tree. Knowledge can be used for good or evil, and places full of information rightly remind learners that knowledge can build up or tear down. Libraries are important to theological education. No discussion of teaching and research is possible without attention to libraries, which function both as teacher and researcher in a theological school. Libraries can be perceived as expensive warehouses for books. They can also be understood as participants in the work of teaching, learning, and research. I am including this discussion because I am committed to the second understanding.

On many ATS campuses, the library is a gathering place for students as well as a source of information. New library buildings have rooms for group study and spaces for interaction. The main entrance to Denver Seminary's new library is through a coffee shop. United Seminary in Dayton has a replica of the Wright Flyer (Wilbur and Orville's father, Bishop Wright, had connections with one of the predecessor seminaries of United), and it will cause people to talk. Theological libraries are about people seeking information and people talking to each other about ideas and information — or the replica of the first heavier-than-air flying machine! These days, talk is abundant in libraries.

Libraries Are about People and Information

The *Chronicle of Higher Education* published an article about Leland Park upon his retirement as director of the E. H. Little Library at Davidson College after thirty-one years of service. Davidson is not a theological school, but it has sent its share of graduates to Columbia and Union seminaries over the years. Park's philosophy of the library is that it should meet the needs of the users. "He has said over and over again, 'The only thing that matters in this library is who walks in that front door.' "[25] The center of good libraries has always been competent, personal service.[26]

During a visit to a school that was applying for ATS membership, I conducted the usual ATS staff visit to the library. Like a majority of applicant schools, the space for the school's library was too limited, the collection was too small, and the small collection had too many books that were gifts from personal collections. When I began to quiz the librarian about the access students had to the other theological collections in the area, given the school's limited holdings, I sensed that I had touched a nerve. My first thought was that she was defensive because students did not have formal borrowing privileges at other libraries. However, that was not it. This librarian was deeply convinced that it was a librarian's job to make sure that a student had the book that was needed; it was not the student's job to go to another library to find it. This librarian did not think the library was good because it had a lot of books on the shelves (which it didn't); she thought it was good because it got any student or faculty member any book he or she wanted, usually in a timely way. Good theological libraries need resources, but in this information age, they need people who have the knowledge and willingness to connect people with the information they need.

As libraries move into the future, there will be more information.

25. Lawrence Biemiller, "Weaving Together Life and Library," *The Chronicle of Higher Education* (19 May 2006): A56. (Phrase sequence slightly revised for clarity.)

26. Many of the ideas in this section on libraries were initially presented at the annual meeting of the American Theological Library Association, June 2006.

The information will become more diffuse, increasingly it will be located in many places or only in digital space, and the paths to access information will become more numerous, more unmediated, more complex, and more mystifying to most persons.

Almost twenty years ago, I visited the University of Oxford for the first time. I went into the Radcliffe Camera of the Bodleian Library. The Camera is primarily a museum room now, but it used to be a place where the collection was held and scholars worked. I looked at the oversized volumes and the way that each was chained to the shelf. There was a time when the library books and building were physically bound together. The books could only be read in the library building. I remember when I was an elementary school student and got my first library card at the town's public library. I found books that I wanted to read and was able to check them out, take them home, and keep them for two whole weeks. There were not many places in my town that let fourth graders walk out the door with things they did not own! It was great. The books weren't chained to the shelves anymore; I had access to a lending library. When my son graduated from college, I took a walk around the campus the day before commencement and stopped by the library, which is a beautiful anchor to the university campus. My son graduated from a teaching university with a beautiful library. Students called it "Club Belk," and they were as likely to meet and chat in the library as in the student center. The library is full of books and stacks, couches and study carrels, meeting rooms and offices. But the most striking feature of the first floor of the library is the computers — rows and rows of flat screens and black keyboards. When I had visited the library, students were always at the computers. Some were accessing the catalog, others were searching databases, some were editing papers, and a lot of them were Instant Messaging (my son told me). Most of the information that can be accessed in this library is not in the form of books that can be checked out, but in databases that give students access to material from all over the world.

Many libraries at ATS member schools are a combination of these three libraries. They have antiquarian and special collections, like the Bodleian at Oxford, with restrictions on access to rare and special volumes. Like my hometown library, they lend their books to students, faculty, and often clergy in the area. All of them have public-access computers. The computers grant access to the Internet, but are used mostly for online catalogs and databases that have either the full text or abstracts of academic articles. The reserve shelf has been augmented by scanned chapters and articles (with proper permissions) that make them simultaneously available to all the students in a course, instead of just one student at a time. Like theological research, libraries change by adding, not by replacing.

Theological Libraries and the Increase of Digital Information

In a 2006 *New York Times Magazine* article, Kevin Kelly wrote: "From the days of Sumerian clay tablets till now, humans have 'published' 32 million books, 750 million articles and essays, 25 million songs, 500 million images, 3 million videos, TV shows and short films, 100 billion Web pages. . . ." (I don't know how Kelly knows all this, but I assume he does.) "When fully digitized, the whole lot could be compressed on to 50 petabyte hard disks."[27] A "petabyte," I read, equals a thousand terabytes, and a terabyte, I read, equals a thousand billion bytes of information. (My use of the word "read" illustrates the difference between reading and understanding!) His point was that the needed petabyte disks could be stored in a building the size of a town library. Most theological books are not yet available digitally, but some are and, in the future, more will be. Some academic presses are considering publishing scholarly monographs only in digital form. The books on library shelves are not disappearing, but the dramatic increase of information will be, increasingly, conveyed and stored in digital form. Theological texts will follow the trend but will not lead it. The leading edge of the trend belongs to subjects that change rapidly, like medicine and technology, and to areas with revenue to pay for the

27. Kevin Kelly, "Scan this Book!" *New York Times Magazine,* 14 May 2006, sec. 6.

transfer from paper to digital texts, like law. Theological monographs do not have large circulation, do not make much money, and usually go out of print before they go out of date. However, as the cost of digitizing material decreases, theological libraries will provide access to more and more digital information.

I have heard librarians express concerns about digital theological texts. Theological discourse is driven by chapters of argument that don't reduce easily to screens of information. Will people read chapters of an argument in a digitized book or just enough screens for part of the argument and a reference?

Whether in books or chips, theological libraries have the same mission — "to provide access to trustworthy, authoritative knowledge."[28] The library has historically controlled for "authoritative and trustworthy" by its collection development and selection of books, and controlled for "access" by organizing, cataloging, and circulating. The library's mission will not change, but the way this mission is achieved will change over time. Jerry Campbell's assessment makes sense to me, and includes several predictions, of which I'd like to make note of two.[29]

First, the more information there is, and the more condensed it is, the more critical guided access will become. I attend a congregation that has Bibles in every pew rack. The order of service prints the book, chapter, and verse for every Scripture passage read in the service, so worshippers can follow along in the pew Bibles. In library language, both the resource (the Bible) and the access information (chapter and verse) are readily available. But for many people, that is not enough. The page numbers of the passages in the pew Bible are printed in the order of worship and, in addition, chapter, verse, and page number are typically announced from the lectern when the Scripture is read. If it takes three kinds of access information for Sunday worshippers to find a text in the pew Bible, imagine how

28. Jerry D. Campbell in "Changing a Cultural Icon: The Academic Library as a Virtual Destination," *Educause* 41, no. 1 (January/February 2006): 16-30 uses this definition for an academic library.

29. Campbell, "Changing a Cultural Icon," pp. 16-30.

much coaching will be needed in a digital library that is a repository of everything that has ever appeared in any form of media in the history of humankind. The more readily information is available, the more complex access actually becomes.

Second, as digitally stored information becomes increasingly accessible, libraries will need to provide more spaces for people to study. John Wilkin, the librarian at the University of Michigan has noted that ". . . we have more than just about any institution in terms of electronic resources available to our users. . . . And yet, at the same time, people are coming to the library in greater numbers. Our gate count goes up, our circulation stays high . . . people come together to use resources."[30] Libraries will increasingly be places of interaction and study, and students and faculty will require more help identifying reliable and trustworthy information, accessing that information, and using it.

Theological libraries play a central role in the tasks of learning, teaching, and research. They have historically fulfilled this role by providing access to information that is reliable and trustworthy. Libraries provide the viewpoints that are not represented among the current faculty. If their collections have been carefully developed, they provide an exposure to the historical work of the church from centuries past as well as exposure to current work from a continent away. If the collection has been carefully constructed, this record from the past will reflect the best of the many translations of ancient and medieval works, as well as the best of the broad range of current research. Good libraries identify and subscribe to the academic databases that will be most helpful to theological study. Much of the learning for ministry requires personal reflection, assessment, and the utilization of life experiences, but learning for ministry also requires careful attention to the witness of others who have made thoughtful assessments in other centuries, in the context of other intellectual systems. The library is the teacher of the grand tradition of the Christian project. Theological learning, teaching, and research cannot occur in isolation of the things that the library "knows."

---

30. "End Result," *The Chronicle of Higher Education* (3 June 2005): A25.

Theological Schools and Teaching, Research, and Libraries

Thus far, you have read my description of theological learning, teaching, research, and libraries. You also know that I believe they are intimately related, mutually beneficial and crucially important for communities of faith. Furthermore, I am convinced that theological schools are not only the best settings to cultivate these interrelated functions, they may be the only ones that can do it well, over time.

Have these functions, while appropriate in a past era, become a luxury in this one? If theological schools in twenty-first century North America had a great deal of money, if Christianity were growing in cultural influence and prestige, and if theological studies were the high status discipline in universities — the conditions that were present when the current forms of theological schools developed in North America — then the cost and effort necessary to maintain them would seem reasonable. However, these conditions are not present. Theological schools do not have a lot of money. If anything, Christianity is losing cultural status and privilege, and scientific inquiry has eclipsed theology by far in status in universities. These conditions pose questions about the viability of the kind of theological scholarship that I am advocating. Have theological schools become a luxury that North American Christianity can no longer afford?

Financially stressed theological schools are making decisions by triage, like emergency department physicians. Does the library get the funding it needs to develop its collection and subscribe to needed databases or does the leaky roof on the classroom building get repaired? Does the vacancy in New Testament get filled or is that budget line used to grant small raises to the rest of the faculty? Does the school support research by keeping teaching loads reasonable or does it increase them to increase productivity? These are not the exceptional decisions that a few schools must make; they are decisions that many schools are being forced to make regularly. These decisions are driven by financial pressure, not educational vision, but their most direct consequences are educational. In tough financial situations, theological scholarship is at risk.

Schools can relieve some of the financial pressure by shifting more teaching from full-time faculty to part-time or adjunct faculty. Adjunct or part-time faculty are typically drawn from nearby undergraduate institutions or congregational ministry settings. These persons enjoy the opportunity to teach a seminary course and, in general, serve theological education very well. Most take their seminary teaching very seriously. Many bring practitioner experience and fresh reports from ministerial practice to the classroom. As theological schools seek to increase access to students who cannot come to campus by expanding the number of extension centers and branch campuses and adding Internet-based educational opportunities, adjunct and part-time faculty become even more essential. Adjunct and part-time faculty are much less expensive than full-time faculty, which is one reason that their number has been rising in theological schools.

While adding more part-time and adjunct instructional staff reduces cost, it also changes theological teaching. Often, the depth with which a subject is understood differs between full- and part-time faculty. Full-time faculty make their living reading, researching, and writing in their areas of specialty while part-time faculty typically have broader occupational pursuits and less time to work in depth in the area they teach. If teaching is primarily the transmission of technical knowledge, like courses on accountancy at the local branch of the University of Phoenix, then there may be very little difference between full-time and part-time teachers. If, however, theological education is about theological understanding pertaining to responsible life in faith, then it requires more than the transmission of information. If teaching in theological schools is about pedagogies of interpretation, formation, contextualization, and performance, which blend and cohere in unique ways within courses and across them, then a predominantly full-time faculty is crucial. Theological education is enriched when supplemented by faculty in other schools and practicing clergy as adjunct and part-time teachers, but its educational capacity would be diminished if finances pushed schools to a predominantly part-time and adjunct faculty.

Research requires institutional settings like theological schools if it is to thrive over time and remain relevant to the larger enterprise of theological education. But is it still needed? Maybe all the books that really need to be written have been written; maybe the canon of viable research, like the canon of sacred Scripture, is now closed. And, if there is any technical research that needs to be completed to update the canon, couldn't it be left to faculty in schools with large endowments or university affiliations that have the resources to make research a priority? Fifty years ago, my parents gave me a Bible, and one of the Scripture verses my dad cited in his inscription was 2 Timothy 2:15, which read, "Study to shew thyself approved unto God, a workman that needeth not to be ashamed, rightly dividing the word of truth." As a fourth grader, I was not sure what "shew" meant, and I had not thought of myself as much of a workman, but I got the point: there is a connection between faithfulness and study. I don't think that Christianity at any age can be faithful without the study necessary for that age, the research that is needed for a particular culture with its particular intellectual systems and perspectives. I don't believe that the Christian project has had all the research it needs. It would be a huge failure if Christians in North America, by most accounts the richest Christians in the past two thousand years, were to conclude that there was insufficient money to support faculty research for this age, for this cultural moment.

The best theological libraries in North America are all associated with theological schools, as are virtually all of the good ones, and most of the modest ones. Libraries are often seen as a very expensive nicety. Most of the books in most of the libraries are never read by most of the faculty members or students, so why keep adding to the stacks? Doesn't the digital age mean that all the needed material will be available electronically? Are libraries worth the amount of the school's budget that they consume? The cost of theological libraries must be taken seriously. When the Association adopted redeveloped accrediting standards, it shifted language from ownership to access. A theological library does not need to purchase books that are already in other nearby libraries if students and faculty have access to those books by shared borrowing agreements. Libraries in nearby theological schools should have coordinated collection development policies to maximize unique holdings and minimize duplication. Subscription to online databases can eliminate the cost of purchasing, binding, and storing paper copies of journals. New initiatives are being considered. Available technology makes it possible for books to be stored at large remote facilities and digitally copied and made available to users upon request. All of these technological changes will enhance the range of literature available for research and reduce some costs, but anyone who has worked with technology in institutions knows that what technology tends to save in one area it costs in another.

The mission of an academic library is to make authoritative and trustworthy information available. The Internet provides access to a huge amount of literature, but it is very difficult to tell what is authoritative and trustworthy. I "Googled" "Luther's Commentary on Romans" as I was working on this paragraph. This is one of Luther's most often consulted commentaries and an important resource for understanding his ideas about justification. The search produced thousands of hits, and even identified sites that have copies available online. This commentary was written five hundred years ago in German. Which, if any, of the online versions is the most reliable and trustworthy translation of early sixteenth-century German into twenty-first-century English? Translations are not exact; they reflect translator interpretations of text and they vary from one another. An Internet search engine can take a reader to sources, but it does not identify which are trustworthy and reliable. It takes a reference librarian, in consultation with expert faculty, to make that judgment. It takes a library, even if the function of the library changes because of the growing amount of literature online.

If theological scholarship involves teaching, learning, and research, as the ATS standards contend, then *schools* are crucial for scholarship. They are one of the few institutions that cultivate all of these activities in relationship with each other, and they can do it with continuity over time.

On a trip to England several years ago, my wife and I drove to Holy Isle. It is a tidal island just off England's northeastern coast.

When the tide is out, cars can get to the island on a causeway, and when the tide is in, the road is covered and Lindisfarne is an island. A monastery was established there as early as 635 C.E., by monks from Iona. They ran a school, copied manuscripts, and advanced manuscript art, of which the most beautiful and widely known are the Lindisfarne Gospels.[31] It was through the work of these and other monks that the multiple copies of Scriptures were made available, and through the school, young men were educated so they could be read and understood. I can imagine someone thinking that a monastery never needs more than one copy of a passage of Scripture, and that the art is too extravagant, and Christianity is too fragile in seventh-century England for elaborately decorated copies of the Gospels. But the monks did their research, taught their students, copied and adorned the texts, and the Scriptures survived the Norman Conquest and other threats. Maybe twenty-first-century Christians should be faithful to the same calling.

31. A brief account of the Lindisfarne Gospels and a picture of a page can be found at The British Library site: www.bl.uk/onlinegallery/themes/euromanuscripts/lindisfarne.html.

CHAPTER 4

Making Theological Schools Work: Governing and Administering

Theological schools have two primary jobs. One is the work of the schools — theological scholarship that includes the interrelated tasks of learning, teaching, and research. The second is making the schools work — attending to the systems of governance and administration. Theological schools have no reason to exist if they are not engaged in the first job, and they won't last long if they aren't engaged in the second. Schools cannot function successfully without effective systems of governance and administration. Across the past twenty years, almost all of the serious accrediting sanctions issued by the ATS Commission on Accrediting have related to failures in governance, administration, or finances, and for many of the schools with sanctions related to finances, the underlying problem had as much to do with governance or administration as financial resources.

Governance and administration have changed dramatically since World War II. Prior to that time, most theological schools were deeply integrated with denominations or church bodies, and many operated more like units that needed management than institutions that needed governance. Other schools functioned more by familial "mom and pop" organizational patterns. Administrative offices were fewer in number and powerful leaders could make things work by dint of personality or sheer personal force. Most theological schools founded since World War II are not related to denominations at all, and many denominational schools are more loosely bound to their parent bodies than they were sixty years ago. Acceptable patterns of leadership are less autocratic and administrative tasks are greater in number. Theological schools inhabit a world of greater accountability to constituent and government entities, increased societal litigiousness, and deeper organizational complexity. All of these changes require schools to develop more formal, often more complex, patterns of governance and administration.

When theological schools do their work well, they constitute the ideal setting in which good theological scholarship can thrive. In order for the schools to do their work well, however, they need thoughtful and effective governance and administration. These tasks are no less important than theological scholarship and require no less intellectual skill and effort.

Governance

Governance is the process by which a theological school makes the decisions that identify and renew the school's mission, implement the mission, and assess the degree to which and the way in which it is being attained. The ATS accrediting standards identify three elements that are necessary for governance in a theological school: authority, structure, and process.

The ATS standards define *authority* as "the exercise of rights, responsibilities, and powers accorded to a theological school by its charter, articles of incorporation and bylaws, and ecclesiastical and civil authorizations. . . ."[1] Trinity Lutheran Seminary in Columbus, Ohio, is related to the Evangelical Lutheran Church in America. It has the authority to receive charitable contributions that are tax deductible because the Internal Revenue Service has formally determined that the school fits the IRS guidelines for nonprofit institutions. It has author-

---

1. Commission on Accrediting, Standard 8, section 8.1, "Authority."

ity to grant degrees because the Ohio Board of Regents has formally granted that authority to the school. It is a seminary of the Evangelical Lutheran Church in America because that denomination has given it the authority to claim this identity. The authority for Trinity to operate comes from these various governmental and ecclesiastical sources; it is not something the seminary gives itself, and it is vested by these various sources in the board of the school.

Structure identifies the entities responsible for the decisions that make the school work. The structure of governance at Trinity Lutheran Seminary, for example, involves many groups. The board makes final decisions about the mission of the school, budget, election of the president, conditions of employment for faculty and staff, and the granting of degrees to graduates. The board delegates authority to the faculty to make decisions about applicants to admit to degree programs, courses to include in the curriculum, the requirements and educational goals of the degree programs, and students who should be granted degrees. Administrative officers are given authority to make decisions about finances, facilities, institutional advancement, attending to the relationship with the Evangelical Lutheran Church in America, and other areas. The seminary includes students in governance, as groups elected by students have authority to make decisions about the allocation of funds for certain student activities and to determine which activities should be funded.

Governance also requires a *process* by which the structure is ordered and implemented. The roles and relationships of various entities need to be clearly defined in procedures and policies. The board at Trinity, for example, grants degrees upon the recommendation of the faculty; the president recommends actions related to initial appointment of faculty, as well as promotion and tenure, with the counsel of the faculty; and the faculty make some decisions about degree requirements — for example, changing the total number of course credits required for a degree — with the concurrence of the board. The structure is implemented by carefully defined processes and procedures that identify which group does what kind of work and how each group's activity is coordinated with that of other groups.

Schools construct their structures and processes in various ways. The ATS standards state that, "While final authority for an institution is vested in the governing board and defined by the institution's official documents, each school shall articulate a structure and process of governance. . . ."[2] The standards go on to enumerate the roles and responsibilities that different entities should assume in the governance process. These policies and procedures are not bureaucratic encumbrances; they are means by which authority flows through the structures to produce governance.

While governance requires many groups, I'd like to focus on the role of governing boards and the ways in which boards should attend to the responsibilities of the president and the faculty in the governance process. (The role of presidents has been thoughtfully described in *A Handbook for Seminary Presidents*.)[3] As I have talked with board members and watched boards in action, I have come to the conclusion that boards are most likely to think that their job is to take action[4] and that they have done their job well when those actions, in retrospect, prove to have been good ones. However, some of the best board meetings may consist of discussions that lead to no decisions at all. Board work involves guiding an institution both by informed decision making and by critical and creative thought.

Governance and Decision Making

The board makes decisions in three broad areas: the school's mission, the overall implementation of that mission, and the degree to which that mission is being attained. Because other entities in a theological

2. Commission on Accrediting, Standard 8, section 8.2.1, "Governance."

3. Robert Cooley, Christa Klein, and Louis Weeks, "The President's Role in Governance," in *A Handbook for Seminary Presidents*, ed. G. Douglass Lewis and Lovett H. Weems Jr. (Grand Rapids: William B. Eerdmans Publishing Company, 2006).

4. The general statements I am making in this section on governance emerge from numerous concrete experiences with governing boards of ATS schools. However, most of these experiences occurred in the context of confidential accrediting interactions, and it would be inappropriate to cite examples, even anonymously.

school make governing decisions related to these areas, the board's decisions are not exclusive, but they are crucial to the overall process.

The mission is what the school understands itself called to do. Most ATS schools have similar elements in their mission statements because they share a common calling. While the schools relate to different ecclesial communities and emphasize different strategies, their work is very similar. Whether Roman Catholic, Evangelical Protestant, Orthodox, or mainline Protestant, they are committed to educating religious leaders, advancing theological understanding, and serving communities of faith. In the 1990s, a church historian evaluated the mission statements of Evangelical and mainline Protestant schools and concluded that there was almost no difference within or between the groups.[5]

Institutional mission is crucial because the vocation of a theological school is a corporate calling. A theological school requires a community of persons to achieve its purposes, including board members, administrators, faculty, students, donors, congregations, and denominational entities. Vocation is typically construed in individual terms, but communities are also called. Some individuals would like an institution to provide a safe and secure setting in which to exercise their individual callings. However, that is not the purpose of a theological school. Its mission is larger than providing the space for individual callings to flourish, although it may include that. The work of a school is not the sum of different individual efforts; it is the work of community effort oriented to a common mission.

Boards do not spend a great deal of time on mission statements, but the task of discerning the mission and refining it in the context of decisions about implementation is crucial to the well-being of the school. A clear understanding of mission keeps boards focused in their guidance. An inadequate focus creates problems. When theological schools stray from their mission, for example, they waste operational

---

5. This conclusion is drawn from an analysis that Paul Basset shared with a study group convened for several years at Fuller Theological Seminary on the aims and purposes of Evangelical theological education.

energy. One ATS school received a bequest of a business and, instead of selling the business and adding the revenue to its endowment, it diverted energy and personnel into running the business. Another ATS school inaugurated a business venture that used the expertise of the faculty. While this strategy has been effective in technologically- and scientifically-focused institutions, it was a money loser for this school. These efforts were not foolish — both were made because they promised needed resources — but they were unrelated to the core mission and diverted energy from accomplishing it. The mission is the compass point to which the school's work should be oriented.

The board spends much of its time making decisions related to implementing the mission. These decisions determine the shape of implementation at a particular time (programs and strategies) and also monitor it (budget and fiscal resources, personnel resources, and program design). Decisions about implementation are potentially a troublesome aspect of governance. Boards can be tempted to move beyond decisions about what an implementation strategy should be and begin trying to manage that strategy. Boards are seldom good managers of institutional strategies, and this temptation almost always leads to intrusion that not only stresses the overall governance system but also results in ineffective management. A school has an administration to manage the implementation of the mission and a faculty to implement the school's primary work of learning, teaching, and research. The board's job is to make final decisions about strategy and then empower and legitimate the work of administrators and faculty to implement it.

Board decision making also involves determining the degree to which, and the ways in which, the mission is being attained. This task presents a major challenge to governing boards. Decisions about the mission of a theological school grow out of theological commitments, shared purposes, and institutional history and vision. They are not made often, and they typically draw from a wide reservoir of agreement. Decisions about strategic direction are usually more open to debate, which makes them more difficult. Assessing the attainment of a school's mission is the most difficult of all. It requires agreed-upon indicators of success and more of a show-me-the-evidence stance by the board than a support-the-school-we-care-about stance. (Schools need their boards to take both of these stances. Almost all of them succeed at the second one, but the first is sometimes missing.) Is a school attaining its mission when its enrollment is full, or budget balanced, or graduates are serving in ministry and other settings that use their seminary studies? Or, could all these indicators be positive and the school still not be attaining its mission? Boards typically spend a great deal of time determining strategic direction and monitoring strategic progress, and less on assessing the attainment of the school's mission.

This description of governance as making decisions about mission, implementation, and effectiveness may seem distant from the experience of many board members of ATS schools. Because many theological schools are chronically stressed financially, boards spend a great deal of time making decisions about finances. Many schools have older facilities in need of repair, renovation, or retrofitting to accommodate current programs. The boards of many ATS schools spend a great deal of time sorting out issues related to facilities. These kinds of decisions show up only once in the foregoing section, and then in parentheses! The omission was deliberate. The mission of theological schools is not to have financial resources or buildings. The mission is about learning, teaching, and research in the context of service to communities of faith, and decisions about finances and facilities are strategies to implement the mission. Sometimes, decisions about facilities and finance become so overwhelming that, *de facto,* the mission of the school becomes institutional survival.

Schools that are not deeply anchored in mission, however, don't accomplish much by surviving. Financially stressed schools tend not to close, though they may merge or morph into some other identity. I am concerned that schools will not have resources to meet their mission, but because the board is looking at finances and not mission, it does not realize that the mission is not being accomplished. Schools can be strong enough to survive but too weak to fulfill their mission. For a theological school, that actually is "a fate worse than death." If boards spent more time on mission and assessment of missional attainment, my hunch is that they would have a much better frame for making decisions about finances and facilities.

Governance and Differing Kinds of Work

Decision making is not the only way to look at board responsibilities. Richard Chait, William Ryan, and Barbara Taylor have provided a helpful and creative way of understanding the work of boards that is very applicable to theological schools. They divide the kind of work that a board should undertake into three categories.[6] The first is the fiduciary care of the school, including its financial assets and organizational policies and procedures. The second is the strategic work of determining how to implement the mission. Many, but not all, of the board's decisions are related to these two areas of work. The third kind of board work is the generative task of identifying the meaning of the school's work and reframing its problems. This last category involves fewer decisions but engages critical and creative thinking in different ways than the first two.

The fiduciary work of the board involves the various decisions and actions of the board that "prevent theft, waste, or misuse of resources; ensure that resources are deployed effectively and efficiently to advance the organization's mission; safeguard the mission against both unintentional drift and unauthorized shifts in purpose; and require that trustees operate solely in the best interests of the organization."[7] The fiduciary work of governing is basic to ensuring the fiscal and missional integrity of the school. It involves each of the kinds of decisions I described above: identifying mission, determining and monitoring the implementation of the mission, and assessing the attainment of mission. Much of the legal liability of an institution is governed by the fiduciary work of boards. Chait and his colleagues also note how fiduciary care attends to the relationship of resources and mission. They

6. Richard P. Chait, William P. Ryan, and Barbara E. Taylor, *Governance as Leadership: Reframing the Work of Nonprofit Boards* (New York: John Wiley & Sons, 2005).

7. Chait et al., *Governance as Leadership*, p. 34.

describe, for example, how the board of a youth-serving agency decided that deteriorated facilities and low salaries meant that the budget had been balanced on the backs of staff and the usefulness of facilities, to the detriment of the long-term mission of the organization. The board's fiduciary responsibility should ensure the attainment of the mission in the context of fiscal and procedural integrity. Fiduciary work is necessary but not sufficient for organizational governance. If a board fails to fulfill its fiduciary role, it fails the school in a very fundamental way. If all the board does is its fiduciary work, it fails the school in other ways.

The second kind of governance work is strategic. Here, the "organization seeks to align internal strengths and weaknesses with external opportunities and threats, all in pursuit of organizational impact."[8] This kind of work recognizes that the world is changing and that schools, however durable and stable they may be, need to reconfigure the strategies they are pursuing to attain their missions. Strategic work is not the same as strategic planning. Chait and his colleagues, in fact, raise serious questions about the technical processes that have become normative for strategic planning. "Rather than rely only on a formal, analytical, and technical process . . . leaders can arrive at strategy another way: through insight, intuition, and improvisation."[9] This kind of board work does not involve reviewing a plan, or the proposals from the president, as much as the board itself thinking about how the school should address its future in the context of external reality and the responses of other schools. Strategic work is creative and improvisational rather than bureaucratic and regulatory. It is a process that looks throughout the organization for good ideas; sometimes the best ideas come from unusual places. This process blurs the lines between board and senior administrators. It calls for partnership as it seeks to construct a "consensus about what the organization's strategy should be."[10] One note of caution: while strategic work means that board

---

8. Chait et al., *Governance as Leadership,* p. 52.
9. Chait et al., *Governance as Leadership,* p. 62.
10. Chait et al., *Governance as Leadership,* p. 69.

members might involve themselves in some focused aspect of the school's work for a period of time, it is crucial that the board avoid micromanaging institutional operations.

The third kind of board work is less prevalent, and in some boards, not present to any observable degree. It is generative governance. Generative work does not result in a better plan or strategy; it results in a better idea — the kind of idea that might lead to new strategies. Generative governance deals with "problem-framing or sensemaking."[11] It involves looking at data and past efforts but seeing that work differently. It involves a shift in paradigm. Thomas Kuhn, a historian of science, notes that scientific paradigms do not shift because of a breakthrough new discovery but because of a new perspective derived from existing data.[12] Ancient scholars thought that the earth was the center of the universe (as it was then understood). Then, in the sixteenth century, Copernicus argued that the sun was the center. He had no data that was not available to other observers; rather, he developed a new idea from the old data. This is generative work. Chait warns against confusing generative work with speculative prediction about the future, and he supports the view that the "power to construct (or reconstruct) the past begets the power to shape the future."[13] Generative work is necessary to identify the meaning and hopes that give rise to the mission. It is not easily planned because it arises from problems and opportunities that do not occur on a regular basis. The board's responsibility is to recognize generative moments and seize them for the worth and value they bring to the rest of its work.

Structures of Institutional Oversight

Governing boards are positioned in many different governing structures in North American theological schools. Four are most typical. The most prevalent is a governing board of a freestanding school that

11. Chait et al., *Governance as Leadership*, p. 84.
12. Thomas Kuhn, *The Structure of Scientific Revolutions*, 2nd ed. (Chicago: University of Chicago Press, 1970).
13. Chait et al., *Governance as Leadership*, p. 88.

has full power and authority to make all decisions related to the school. Board members are elected by a sponsoring denomination, by the board itself, or by some combination of both. Once elected, the board has full authority to govern the school. In a second pattern, typically Roman Catholic, a bishop or religious order legally owns the school but appoints a board. In some cases, the appointed board is advisory, and in others, it has decision-making power in designated areas. In the third pattern, a theological school is an integrated unit of a college or university, is governed through the administrative structures of the larger institution, and is accountable to the larger institution's board. Many of these schools have advisory boards, but they typically have little power related to finance, program, legal, or employment issues. A fourth pattern — once characteristic of many schools in Canada — is bicameral. One body (predominantly persons not employed by the institution) has full responsibility for fiscal, property, and corporate issues, while another (usually predominantly faculty) has full responsibility for curriculum and academic programs. Neither body has authority over the other. This model has dissipated over the years as financial decisions needed to be closely coordinated with educational and program decisions. Most Canadian schools now have unicameral boards.

Though structures vary, each theological school has a formalized process by which decisions are made about its mission, implementation of strategies, and assessment regarding overall missional effectiveness.

Trust and Shared Governance

Whatever its structure of governance, trust is the most crucial asset for effective governance of a theological school. The ATS standard on governance begins: "Governance is based on a bond of trust among boards, administration, faculty, students, and ecclesial bodies."[14] If the board does not trust the administration or the faculty, no set of governing policies and procedures will effectively guide the school. If the

---

14. Commission on Accrediting, Standard 8, "Authority and Governance."

faculty does not trust the board and administration, the mission that the board may dictate may not be the mission that will be implemented, course by course. Not all systems of governance assume trust as a basic condition. A military command and control structure, for example, is based on obedience and execution. It is designed to work even when trust breaks down. When trust is lacking in theological schools, however, governance breaks down. The corporate life of the institution may be sustained but not its missional vitality. Trust is crucial, and it appears to exist in abundance in ATS schools. For example, the Auburn Center for the Study of Theological Education conducted a major study of trustees of ATS schools and found that the climate of trust between the board and the chief executive officer was exceptionally high.[15]

Trust is so crucial because theological schools operate with systems of shared governance. This is by far the most unique aspect of governance in higher education institutions. Shared governance is a highly valued but often misunderstood concept. Its definition varies by institution as each college or university develops and implements its own policies by which shared governance is exercised. There is no formal understanding, for example, of the structure of shared governance or the role of faculty within it. Most institutional policies involve participation by faculty, administrators, and sometimes students and graduates. Most involve patterns of information sharing. In all cases, shared governance is defined by each school's policies and procedures.

The ATS standards reflect this broader reality in higher education by acknowledging that "Each institution should articulate its own theologically informed understanding of how this bond of trust becomes operational as a form of shared governance."[16] Roman Catholic seminaries, for example, are subject to canon law, as well as to the *Program of Priestly Formation* adopted by the Conference of Catholic

---

15. This figure is part of a study that is reported in Barbara G. Wheeler, "In Whose Hands: A Study of Theological School Trustees," *Auburn Studies*, no. 9 (June 2002 [July 2002]).

16. Commission on Accrediting, Standard 8, "Authority and Governance."

Bishops, and no pattern of shared governance within the seminary can countermand governance expectations contained in these normative documents. Within these formal guidelines, however, Catholic seminaries can have systems of shared governance. A freestanding Protestant seminary, with no canonical accountabilities, is able to develop systems of shared governance without external constraint. College- and university-related theological schools are bound by the understanding of shared governance exercised by the larger institution of which they are a part.

Given the variation across theological schools, is there an overarching framework within which shared governance can be understood? The ATS standards have a strategy: "each school shall articulate a structure and process of governance that appropriately reflects the collegial nature of theological education. . . . Shared governance follows from [this] collegial nature. . . ."[17] Shared governance begins with the board's authority and continues by distributing decision making across many entities within the school, through a properly defined and coordinated system. Consider, for example, a freestanding theological seminary with a fully empowered board. The board has the legal authority to make every decision related to the school's operation. It can decide which degree programs will be offered, what the curriculum will be for each program, who the faculty of instruction will be, which students to admit, which standards of conduct are expected of students, what constitutes acceptable student performance, and any other decision that is part of the school's operation. While boards have this authority, they do not keep the authority in a board-only governance model. Typically, they *share* it. In most ATS schools, the board typically approves the offering of degree programs, but grants governing power to the faculty for determining the curriculum and degree requirements, the admission of students to the program, and the acceptable level of performance necessary to earn the degree. Because the meaning of shared governance varies, it is crucial that schools develop formally adopted procedures and guidelines that de-

---

17. Commission on Accrediting, Standard 8, sections 8.2.1 and 8.2.2.

fine roles and responsibilities for each entity involved in the governance process. Because shared governance involves the work of many partners, it is crucial that the procedures be followed carefully and intentionally.

Shared governance acknowledges that theological scholarship — the work of the schools — is not the kind of activity that can be governed in a top-down fashion. Most board members don't know what scholarly books need to be written, or which courses need to be revised, or which students should be dismissed from study. Both the collegial nature of a theological school and the nature of its work make shared governance necessary rather than elective. Shared governance means that governing structures in theological schools differ in very significant ways from governance structures in most corporations. Board members who are accustomed to corporate governing structures — even ones that encourage team-oriented approaches to management — find shared governance a strange pattern. Properly implemented, it strengthens schools and maximizes their potential to attain their missions.

Over the years, I have seen three models in which shared governance has been implemented in ATS schools. In one, the board, the faculty, (and sometimes the administration through the president), all vote on an issue — like recommending a new member of the faculty or electing a new president. The new faculty member is appointed or new president elected only if all entities vote affirmatively. While this model shares governance and invites participation of the major entities in the school, it results in giving each entity effective veto power. I have observed cases where this model brought theological schools to a virtual standstill when there were deep differences between faculty and board. It is not an effective model of shared governance.

Another model I have observed divides decision making into zones and gives different entities governing authority within each zone. A freestanding seminary where the board approves the offering of degree programs and the faculty determines curriculum and degree requirements is an example of the second model. It works well when all entities understand and respect the boundaries in the governing zones and when the entity responsible for a zone of governance has expertise in that area.

A third model is interactive. The board, for example, grants degrees, but only upon the recommendation of the faculty. The board takes final action to promote faculty from one rank to another or to grant tenure, but it takes these actions only upon the recommendation of the president, who typically makes his or her recommendation after consulting with the faculty via some formal procedure. A president may make a recommendation about a faculty member that the faculty has not supported, or fail to make one that the faculty did support, but does so only cautiously.

None of these models presupposes that the faculty has an intrinsic or corporate right to govern, even in areas of its greatest expertise. Governance begins and ends with the board. Good governance, however, requires sharing the process to maximize the expertise that informs decisions and ownership of their results. Most theological schools have shared governance structures that reflect both the second and third models.

Shared governance is not easy and can be problematic. While all versions must acknowledge the final authority of the board, each model introduces ambiguity into the governing process. As regulatory and litigious demands increase, decisions made by the faculty could result in costly litigation, which would pressure boards to review the extent to which they are willing to share governance with faculty. Also, shared governance systems are slower than almost any other form of governance. This is not a problem in times of stability, but in transitional times, when schools must move quickly in new directions, the slow pace of shared governance systems is a hindrance. Shared governance can be abused by parties in the school when they use their role to impede or undermine the progress of the institution.

The benefits of shared governance, like many other characteristics of theological schools, are not always visible but powerfully impact the implementation of the school's mission. The mission of a school is delivered most directly by the faculty. Graduating students identify faculty, by far, as the most influential aspect of their theological education.[18] The reputation of most theological schools is borne by the faculty and, almost without exception, it is enhanced by them. Faculty members have considerable expertise about subject areas and how students learn them, and they can make many educational decisions better than any other group in the institution. Faculty must have a stake in determining the educational goals and purposes of the school because they directly implement the mission. Given their influence on attaining the school's mission, sharing appropriate governance with faculty can advance the highest goals of the school.

Governance Failures

Good governance does not make a great school, but a school cannot be great without it. As governance grows in importance, failures in governance become increasingly problematic. ATS accreditation has noted three categories of failure in governance that have led to institutional turmoil and instability and, in turn, to formal accreditation sanctions.

The first is when the board ignores or fails to follow institutional policy. In most ATS schools, the board governs through formally adopted policies and procedures by which it does its own work and orders that of the faculty and administration. There are times, however, when the board wants to accomplish some action and the procedures it has adopted seem awkward or too circuitous, and it acts contrary to procedures. This can be disastrous for a school. Other times, procedures and policies have been formally adopted and forgotten — either because the members who adopted the policy have rotated off the

18. The ATS *Entering Student Questionnaire* asks students to identify the most important factors in their decision to attend the institution in which they have just enrolled. Of the fifteen options given, the two chosen by almost every entering group of students is "faculty" or "academic reputation of the school," which is closely linked to the faculty. The ATS *Graduating Student Questionnaire* asks students to identify the three most important influences in their theological education. From a list of eighteen possible influences, graduates chose "faculty" more frequently, by far, than any of the other potential influences. For the most recent data from both questionnaires, see www.ats.edu/Resources/Student/Pages/default.aspx.

board or they adopted the policy without understanding it. Few things destabilize an institution more than failure to develop appropriate governing policies or to follow those that have been adopted. If the board cannot be trusted to follow its own procedures, governance becomes unpredictable and *ad hoc,* susceptible to the pressures and preferences of powerful members or impromptu demands.

A second problem that schools may experience is boards paying too little attention to the critically important issues. Financial reports are complex and reading institutional audits can be difficult for people who are not experienced with financial statistics. Most members of the boards of ATS schools are on the board because they care deeply for the school or the denomination that has elected them. They approach their work with support and appreciation for the school. Good-hearted and high-minded persons can fail to see financial warning signs or institutional trouble. Board members are in board meetings two or three times a year and, unless they pay close attention, they may miss indicators that the institution is under threat in some way. It is important for the board to pay attention, ask hard questions, and both support the administration and hold it accountable.

The third problem is the inverse of the second: intrusive attention in the operation of the school. A board is an excellent governing body, but a poor managing one. There are times when the school needs the unique expertise and insight of board members, or when generative and strategic tasks call the board, faculty, and administration into creative partnerships; but the board, as a whole, does not have sufficient information for close operational decisions. Senior executives and business owners on the boards of ATS schools certainly know a great deal about operations and management, but as board members, they should limit their role to board decisions and not try to run the seminary as they would their corporations or businesses. Likewise, clergy board members can't run a seminary as they would their congregations. Sometimes the board as a whole shifts from governance to management, and sometimes it is an individual who attempts to use his or her role on the board to leverage individual power. In either case, the result is almost always negative for the school.

The importance of good board work is increasing, and I have a growing concern about boards. It is not about failure, or lack of goodwill or support for the school, or lack of good sense or thoughtful decisions. Rather, I am concerned about their capacity to do what schools today need them to do. Good as the boards of ATS schools are, the growing significance and complexity of governing processes is outpacing the development of needed governing skills.

Consider the difference between seminary governance in 1950 and 2000. In 1950, most ATS schools were tightly related to one denomination: students belonged to the school's denomination before coming to seminary and would serve in that denomination afterward, the denomination funded a significant portion of the school's operating budget, and board members also belonged to the denomination, regardless of how they were elected. Often, boards were comprised predominantly of clergy, many of whom had attended the seminary. Much has changed. In 2000, most denominations supported a far smaller percentage of a school's operating budget, and finding needed resources consumed a great deal of institutional effort. Students typically came from many denominations and, frequently, so did board members. Furthermore, fewer board members were clergy, which means that fewer knew theological education from the inside.

These changes are only the beginning. The regulatory climate and legal expectations of nonprofit institutions are dramatically different from fifty years ago. It is not clear to me if the governing skills of boards have increased commensurate with the power and responsibility that boards now carry in many theological schools. The United States and Canada have a system of voluntary boards. Unlike corporate governance, members of ATS school boards are not compensated and, at some schools, they even pay for their own transportation to the meeting. The competence of individual board members is not at issue — boards are full of talented people. Individual competence is not enough, however. Boards also need sophisticated practices and skills as boards. These are necessary for both good decision making and the critical and creative thought that governance today requires.

Administration

For several years, I participated with a dozen colleagues in an annual weekend meeting. Most of us had planned to become academic researchers and teachers and we were all in administrative jobs — agency executives, seminary presidents, religious publishing executives. Most of us had been seminary faculty members earlier in our careers, and we wondered if, somehow, we had abandoned our callings to serve in our current jobs. Over the course of our summer conversations, we discussed the intellectual issues that are involved in doing our work well, and to the extent that we came to a conclusion, it was that administrative leadership requires as much intellectual effort as the teaching and research we had done earlier, maybe more.

Growth and Importance of Administration

Administration has grown steadily in ATS schools. Where there was no development officer in many schools forty years ago, there is now a development staff. Where there may have been a dean of students with a secretary years ago, there is now a staff to support the range of needs of a very different kind of student body. Where there may have been a treasurer with an accounting clerk, there is now a staff. No one was dealing with information technology forty years ago; now most schools have at least one IT professional. Fifty years ago, most schools did not have a recruitment office, now most could not exist without one. Then, communications involved keeping the denomination well informed, and an assistant in the president's office could do that. Now, the school has to work hard to tell its story to a wide range of audiences. All administrative functions in theological schools are more complex than they were fifty years ago.

In the 2005-06 academic year, ATS schools spent a total of 33 percent of Educational and General Expenditures (all expenses except those related to auxiliary costs such as housing and food service) on institutional and academic administration,[19] a figure that has been consistent across the past five years. Although ATS schools tend to be small, relative to other higher education institutions, they require all the same administrative offices as larger schools. Their size does not help them administer less expensively; administrative functions in smaller schools comprise a higher percentage of expenditures. Administration is important to the success of theological schools, and it both deserves and needs to be well done.

Administrative work provides the institutional care that schools need in order for learning, teaching, and research to thrive. It requires intelligence about getting things done in a way that serves the institution's mission and supports the work of the faculty, students, and other constituents. Administrative work differs from academic scholarship because it uses a broader range of intelligence. It involves the ability to read people as well as policies, a sense about how processes work — and how they are adjusted for institutional or interpersonal needs — and the ability to get things done. In the culture of theological schools, administrative work is best done in ways that include appropriate patterns of participation by faculty, students, and other administrators.

While a seminary requires several senior administrative offices to do its work, I want to focus on the work of the president. In small institutions, the president fills a unique role that both guides and embodies the work of the school, and the administration is, in many ways, an extension of the chief administrator's office. As I have watched presidents of theological schools, I have decided that their work involves three equally important dimensions: alignment with the values and culture of the school, ability to manage, and willingness to lead.

19. These data are from the ATS Annual Report Form information database, and they can be viewed at www.ats.edu/SiteCollectionDocuments/AnnualDataTables/2006-07AnnualDataTables.pdf.

Fit with the Values and Culture of the School

Theological schools are unique environments. While they share much in common, they are deeply different in very particular ways. An American church historian once said that theological schools are "tribal," and I think that is accurate. These schools are communities of particular values and religious commitments, and they form institutional cultures that are more intense than is characteristic of most other higher education institutions. Presidents of theological schools need not only fit into this culture, they need to be *of* it, to bear it. Good administrative leadership is thus not just a function of competent professional skills that are well exercised. Although especially true for the president, the capacity to fill most senior roles in theological schools begins with the individual understanding and honoring the religious center of the school and its long cultural traditions.

The cultural "fit" I am trying to describe is more than a general fit with ethos and organizational culture that is necessary for administrative leadership in most institutional settings. A conservative Baptist seminary is highly unlikely to have a liberal Roman Catholic priest as president or dean — not because he lacks the skills, nor because he doesn't value what the Baptists are seeking to do in their seminary, but because he does not embody the seminary's particular pattern of being Christian; he is not *of* the religious culture of the school. Good seminary leaders are not necessarily icons of the religious and value center of the school; but many of the best ones are. Theological schools are rarified, value-laden environments, and presidents and other senior leaders must embody those values. In a major study of chief academic officers of ATS schools, Jeanne McLean found that some of the most successful deans had come from the faculties of the schools they were currently serving as deans.[20] I suspect they were successful because they both knew the culture and were already part of it. A study of new presidents of ATS schools conducted by the Auburn Center for the

---

20. Jeanne P. McLean, *Leading from the Center: The Emerging Role of the Chief Academic Officer in Theological Schools* (Atlanta: Scholars Press, 1999).

Study of Theological Education supports this conclusion.[21] A theological school has a strong cultural ethos, that ethos is deeply driven by religious values, and those values tend to be broadly shared by faculty and board, which makes the culture all the more powerful. Few other higher education institutions have the unique values-driven culture of theological schools.

Effective Managers

This unique fit to the particular culture of the theological school is necessary but not sufficient for good administrative leadership. Presidents need to be good managers. Rita Bornstein, former president of Rollins College, undertook a study of presidential failures and identified six areas that contributed either to their success or failure.[22] One threat to presidential success, she noted, is managerial incompetence. Schools need good management from the president and other senior administrators. ATS schools cannot be unmanaged or mismanaged very long. I have known a few senior leaders who have failed because of managerial incompetence, but more typically, I have watched schools slide toward weakened capacity because they were not managed carefully.

An institution's employees need to be held accountable, even when it is difficult. Many seminary administrators have been pastors and tend to bring pastoral sensitivities into personnel issues, which provide good attention to personal needs of employees but do not serve the institution well as a supervisory style. Good personnel management understands that a school is an employee environment, not the volunteer environment of a congregation. People need to perform, and sadly, sometimes they need to be let go. Institutional finances need to be managed carefully. Theological schools cannot spend more money than they receive for very long without seriously eroding their ability

---

21. Auburn panel preliminary findings.

22. Rita Bornstein, "The Nature and Nurture of Presidents," *The Chronicle of Higher Education* (4 Nov. 2005), www.chronicle.com/weekly/v52/i11/11b01001.htm.

to fulfill their missions, and they can't spend money inappropriately without jeopardizing the legal status of the school. Managerial competence includes managing money well. Institutions also need good decision-making processes. If reasonable ones exist, they should be followed; if they don't exist, they need to be developed. Good management does not necessarily make a school stronger, but bad management almost always makes it weaker.[23]

Management is about making day-to-day decisions that serve the present needs of the school and, little by little, strengthen the school's future. It is about accomplishing the tasks that need to be done, in ways that honor the policies and procedures that reflect the accrued wisdom of the school about its work, while also making changes that are necessary to extend that wisdom. Sometimes, presidents are tempted to think their most important responsibility is to make the right decision about the truly great issue that will set the school or program on a new course. Management requires an occasional big decision, but most days, it requires a series of good small decisions and actions.

One of my favorite commentators on the human condition is Garrison Keillor. In an article he wrote following Arnold Schwarzeneger's election as governor of California, he commented: "You go for a walk on a summer night and notice the little ramps carved into curbs at street corners. People sat through a lot of meetings to get that accomplished. It was a boon to the wheelchair crowd and also to parents pushing strollers and kids riding bikes. It made life slightly more civil and friendly. Government works through small, incremental changes. . . ."[24] For the most part, administration works the same. Daily decisions and small actions, when made thoughtfully and done well, constitute the work of management. Theological schools grow stronger over time — not so much by the great decision or the great

---

23. One helpful resource for seminary administrators is chapter 2, "The President's Role in Administration and Personnel Management" in *A Handbook for Seminary Presidents*, ed. G. Douglass Lewis and Lovett H. Weems Jr. (Grand Rapids: Eerdmans, 2006).

24. Garrison Keillor, "Hey, Arnold! This Is Serious Stuff," *Time*, 25 Aug. 2003, www.time.com/time/printout/0,8816,1005491,00.html.

gift, but by a consistent and persistent commitment to mission and quality, decision after decision, task after task, year after year.

As communities of value and meaning, theological schools are deeply influenced by abstract ideals like religious commitments and philosophies of education. Management oversees the translation of these abstractions into concrete action. Sometimes, seminaries function as if they could be managed by their ideals. When I was a professor, I walked into the faculty lounge one day when a conversation was under way about a graduate who had just resigned from a pastorate because of sexual misconduct. One of the professors expressed his surprise about the failure because the graduate was such a good theologian. This is not an atypical reaction in a theological school, and it has an impact on seminary management. Too often, administrative work in theological schools is judged by the values of the worker rather than the behavior of the work. In the end, management is about actions and behaviors.[25] It is not enough that a person claims the values of the school or wants to do the right thing. Ultimately, an institution depends on good decisions being made, appropriate actions being taken, and employees being held accountable to do their jobs effectively. These decisions and behaviors need to be exercised by persons who identify with the commitments and philosophy of the school, but there is no direct relationship between holding the values that are widely shared in the school and engaging in effective managerial behavior and decisions.

Good Leadership

Good administration also requires leadership. Robert Terry, one of many thoughtful writers about leadership, puts it simply: leadership involves getting an institution from one point to another.[26] If a school

25. Leslie Wilk Braksick, a consultant and executive coach and also trustee at Princeton Theological Seminary, describes the behavioral dimensions of organizational leadership in *Unlock Behavior, Unleash Profits,* 2nd ed. (New York: McGraw-Hill, 2007).

26. Robert W. Terry, *Authentic Leadership: Courage in Action* (San Francisco: Jossey-Bass, 1993).

is exactly where it needs to be and has no desire to go anywhere else, it doesn't need leadership. It can do very well with managerial caretakers. Most theological schools need to get somewhere, however, and they need leaders. My work has given me the opportunity to watch presidential leaders at work in ATS schools, and many of them have been wonderful, even exceptional. They have helped schools through crises, led them through needed change, and nurtured new understandings of mission and purpose.

Like governance, leadership is almost always shared in a theological school. The president has a leadership role, as do the board, faculty, and, in many seminaries, ecclesial authorities. Leadership must be coordinated, of course, oriented to common purposes. In a day in which the successful corporate leader can become a guru for business, and the successful megachurch pastor an icon for ministry, leadership is heavily personalized. I have heard search committee members say that their school needs a leader who can cast a vision for the school. It sounds as if they want a leader who, like Moses, can go up the mountain, get a word from the Lord, and return to the school with the right vision of what it should do. I don't think that is a viable model of leadership for ATS schools, and I am very sure that vision seldom emerges in this way.[27] Leadership in the context of theological education guides the school in identifying the vision it should pursue and orchestrates the multiple tasks necessary to implement it. It does not merely enable schools to get where they need to go if and when they decide to go somewhere. Institutions need leaders who function catalytically, who can unite different elements around a common cause, empower them to do together what they could not do alone, and orchestrate the processes necessary to achieve change. In this way, change happens in an institution that would not happen without leadership.

Good leaders are motivated by the challenges a school faces, and they see their primary job as addressing these challenges. In conversa-

27. Leith Anderson makes this point in "Vision — See the Goal and Show the Way," chap. 13 in *Leadership That Works: Hope and Direction for Church and Parachurch Leaders in Today's Complex World* (Bloomington, Minn.: Bethany House, 1999).

tions with members of search committees of financially stressed institutions, I have been asked when or if presidential candidates should be told how deep and pressing the financial challenges actually are. My response is that the problems should be among the first things discussed with candidates. The question suggests a fear that telling the truth will drive the best candidates away. In reality, the best candidates will be the ones who are most challenged by the financial stress, want to tackle it, and have some idea of how to address the problem. Max De Pree has said that the first job of a leader is to name reality. Good leaders are energized by reality, not by wishful thinking about what the school could be or used to be. They are motivated by the problems the school is facing, and the possibility that lies beyond their resolution. Leaders see reality in an institution, name it in a way that the constituencies understand, and help the institution see beyond the present difficulties. Ron Heifetz reminds us that leadership usually does not have easy answers and that formulaic understandings of leadership are likely not reliable guides.[28] Leadership is often about guiding institutions through complex problems and needed change. Good leaders don't seek difficulty, but when it comes, they are energized by it and have a way of motivating others in the institution to be energized as well.

Good leaders are characterized by personal humility and intense professional will. That is not my assertion; it is the conclusion of business scholar Jim Collins and his colleagues, derived from their research with publicly held companies that broke ahead of other companies in the same segment and sustained their relative leadership position for fifteen years. This influential study has been widely quoted, and while not all characteristics associated with effective leadership of a publicly held company translate to a theological school, I think at least two do, and they do so readily. Collins and his colleagues interviewed senior executives who were active with these companies as they surged ahead

28. See Ronald A. Heifetz, *Leadership Without Easy Answers* (Cambridge, MA: Belknap Press of Harvard University Press, 1994) and Ronald A. Heifetz and Marty Linsky, *Leadership on the Line: Staying Alive through the Dangers of Leading* (Boston: Harvard Business School Press, 2002).

and as they worked to sustain their relative position over the years. The interviews revealed that these leaders were humble. They worked hard, enjoyed their jobs, and did not define themselves by the perks they received or use their positions to promote personal fame. In the world of celebrity CEOs, it came as a surprise that the CEOs of fifteen of these very successful companies were virtually unknown. Collins also describes them as people of "intense professional will." They were passionate about their companies. They were more committed to their company's achievement over the long term than to personal status. I cannot think of a better pair of qualities for leaders in theological education than personal humility and strong professional will. I have seen it in some of the best leaders of these schools, and when they have retired or moved to another position, they have left stronger and more effective institutions.

Apparently, there were no secret practices that made these successful companies break ahead of their segment and sustain that leadership position over a long term — other than good decisions, made over time, and the institutional discipline to make the decisions work. The descriptions of these companies don't read as if any of them had a strategic plan to become great. Their institutional goals were to find what they did well and what the market needed to have done better. These companies were not afraid to change; they feared stagnation. Collins argues that the enemy of great is good, and the companies identified in this study as most successful were no longer content to be good. They seemed to have been guided more by a drive to improve than a goal to become great and to be discontent with any performance other than their best.

The CEO of one of the companies in this study was Coleman Mockler of the Gillette Corporation. During his tenure, Collins concluded that Gillette underwent three serious hostile takeover attempts and, with each, "Mockler did not capitulate, choosing instead to fight for the future greatness of Gillette, even though he himself would have pocketed a substantial sum on his own shares." As Collins describes Mockler, his placid persona hid an inner intensity, a dedication to making anything he touched the best that it could possibly be — not just because of what he would get, but because he simply couldn't imagine doing it any other way.[29] Coleman Mockler and his wife, Jo Anna, have been generous contributors to Gordon-Conwell Theological Seminary, and after Coleman's death, Jo Anna served as chair of the seminary's board of trustees. Mockler represented the kind of leadership that makes great companies *and* theological schools: a dedication to the best because he could not imagine it any other way.

Good Administration

Higher education is replete with language about excellence. No school wants to be known for mediocre academic work, and few are. However, schools are sometimes not as concerned about mediocrity in governance and administration. ATS schools are not poorly run, but many are not as well run as they would be if schools were as concerned about excellence in governance and administration as they are in academics. An institution cannot effectively pursue excellence if only the president and senior administrators are committed to the goal. It takes broad-based commitment. It requires tracking information about quality so improvement can be noted. It especially takes the commitment of the board. Most institutions require prompting, pushing, and nudging to seek excellence in administration and governance.

Most ATS schools are not competitors with one another. Students choose seminaries primarily because of their location and theological perspectives. While schools of the same denomination are in friendly competition, and some schools of similar theological orientation in the same locale are in competition, it is minimal compared to the competition among baccalaureate degree granting institutions. In North American free-market education, competition is often the incentive for schools to improve. It was certainly the reason the companies in Jim Collins's study improved. Absent competitive incentives, theological schools have to reach inside themselves for motivation. Given the

29. Jim Collins, *Good to Great* (New York: HarperCollins Publishers Inc., 2001), pp. 23-25.

values-driven nature of theological schools, and their goal of service to important issues, schools should be able to identify and nurture an internal spark of excellence. The mission of The Association of Theological Schools is the "enhancement and improvement" of theological schools, and over the years I have observed schools "required" to improve because of an accrediting action. But theological schools will not improve as much as they should, or in the ways they should, if they limit their motivation to external pressure or enticement. It has to be internal. A deep sense of stewardship will push these schools toward change. An abiding commitment to serve well will prompt them toward improvement. An unshakable devotion to the religious commitments of these schools will nudge them toward excellence. Administration is the work of running schools well in ways that both get them through the week and make them better next year.

Good administration faces two threats in theological schools. The first is the tendency of academic institutions to undervalue administrative work. This is the issue that my colleagues and I were dealing with in those summer meetings: is administrative work a good use of academic training and talent? We were asking ourselves the question because it was asked of us by friends and colleagues. We decided that it was, but schools are full of people who are not so sure. Undervaluing administrative work has consequences. Talented people who should be engaged in academic administration decline because they have been convinced that it is an inappropriate use of their education and ability. Or, they take an administrative job for a while as a service to the institution but leave before they have gained the experience to be truly expert in their work. As people rotate through administrative positions in this way, the work is done adequately but without the expertise that contributes to institutional and educational advancement.

The second threat to administration in theological schools is the relatively low compensation scales in most ATS schools. This is not as much a problem for faculty as it is for those administrative functions that truly compete for talent in an open marketplace, such as chief financial or chief development officers. Few people work at theological schools because of economic incentives, but in some administrative offices, compensation ranges at ATS schools can be a significant handicap to attracting people with the needed talent. Theological schools have been fortunate in finding people sufficiently committed to the mission of the school to accept less compensation than they could earn in other settings. Some schools likely have had less talented executive leadership in some of these areas than they needed.

Making Schools Work

Not much has been written on the governance and administration of theological schools. Educational programs in support of theological school governance and administration have emerged only in the past quarter century. Making schools work, however, is becoming both more complex and more critical. Fortunately, members of governing boards give considerable wisdom, as well as time and treasure, to these schools. Fortunately, good senior administrators are serving these schools, even though compensation is not as high as it would be in other sectors of higher education. If the future of theological education is to benefit from schools that provide the ideal setting for the kind of learning, teaching, and research that the church most needs, then making the schools work is absolutely essential.

CHAPTER 5

The Future of Theological Schools: The Church and Higher Education

During the eighteen years that David Tiede was president of Luther Seminary, Luther's denomination merged with two other Lutheran denominations to form the Evangelical Lutheran Church in America. He led the seminary through many changes that accompanied the formation of the new church body, the rethinking of the school's mission, and the strategy for attaining that mission. In the process, Tiede concluded that the historical development of Luther Seminary could be understood in three phases: abbey, academy, and apostolate. He learned that the seminary needed to incorporate all three phases into its mission to serve the church.

The abbey phase of the seminary's history was a time when it was tightly and internally related to a Scandinavian immigrant church. It was faithful to the church, it educated the church's clergy, and it served the church's needs. The seminary was a place of study, prayer, and preparation for ministry. It was a school, but it perceived itself to be an organization of the church more than an institution of higher education. The academy phase emerged as the seminary moved beyond its insular beginnings. It became more like a higher education institution: faculty credentials improved and their research was increasingly valued and expected, the library expanded, and overall the school focused more on academics. It began a Ph.D. program, and faculty participation in academic societies increased. The seminary maintained a close relationship to the church, but its identity shifted. Tiede concluded, however, that the future of the school required movement to a third phase, an apostolate. The seminary needs to understand itself not just as a higher education institution whose mission is to provide graduate, professional theological education, but also — and perhaps more so — as part of Christianity's mission to propagate the gospel. North American culture is less Christian than in the past and, as a religious movement, Christianity needs centers of authority that sustain the Christian message and prepare pastors who can lead congregations to share the gospel in a culture that knows less about Christianity and is not convinced of its value. This is a new and different challenge. It is not a return to the abbey, which was internally focused. It is not an abandonment of academic work. Rather, it is taking academic work in an apostolic direction. The model that David Tiede proposes for Luther Seminary is true for many, if not most, denominational seminaries.

Change in theological schools, as I observed earlier in this essay, tends not to consist of ceasing to be one thing and becoming another. Instead, change resembles tree growth: new rings are added without discarding the old ones. Tiede's abbey, academy, and apostolate are, in some ways, sequential stages of institutional identity, but unlike truly sequential changes, they represent layers of identity and practice that never completely disappear. Luther Seminary continues to be an abbey in certain ways, and an academy, and it is learning to become an apostolate. A seminary gains new identities without losing old ones, and that is both a blessing and a curse. It is a blessing because it gives a school a wide repertoire of skills as it faces different challenges. It allows a theological school to gain wisdom about institutional practice and maintain connections with its past. Historic facilities, tenure, endowments, library collections, respect for institutional history — these are all assets that encourage stability and long-term continuity of educational effort. Difficulties arise, however, when a school's various constituents favor one identity over another or disagree about which model deserves the highest priority. Holding multiple identities and maintaining practices from each phase can also be an impediment to making needed changes as a school strives toward its future.

What is the future of seminary-based theological education? This is a time in North American society when much is changing. It is most obvious in business and medicine, but evident in other cultural institutions, like higher education and religion. The change is deep, pervasive, and marks a turn from the way things have been. Theological schools will need to adapt, but change is precarious business. Premature institutional change can be costly. Changing too late can be disastrous. Refusing to change at all could spell institutional death. The future of theological schools will, in many ways, be defined by the ways in which schools are shaped by and respond to changes in the church, higher education, and the Christian movement as it advances in the twenty-first century. Schools will need to continue their abbey-like role as they carefully attend to the ecclesial communities with which they relate most closely, but the abbey may look different as their communities of faith change. Schools will continue to be academies, but they too will respond to changes in higher education. Schools will further need to develop their identities as apostolates, because the status of Christianity is changing in North America and growing with vigor in much of the two-thirds world. This chapter explores each of these areas of change.

Abbey: Theological Schools and the Church

For twelve years, I taught at a denominational seminary in an era of considerable denominational stress, and the seminaries became symbols of what was thought to have gone wrong in the denomination. During those years, as it had been for much of its history, this seminary was a strong school. It had a dynamic and able student body and a talented faculty that was committed both to the denomination and to the broader world of scholarship. In other ways, the seminary was weakened by the conflict. It was a decade in which a cloud was on the horizon, if not directly overhead. We had a faculty development event one year in which we were divided into groups with the assignment to design a new seal for the seminary. My group came up with a modification of the old ship of faith: it was a submarine with sails, and the motto inscribed around the image was "faithful and flexible."

While I was never a target, the battle always felt close, and one year, the junior high youth at one church made it personal. I was asked to write a curriculum unit for Sunday night youth groups, and in it I wrote a passing comment that the story of the Good Samaritan — the assigned text for the lesson — may have been told as a parable or may have been the account of an actual event. I went on to write that whether it was a parable or actual event, Jesus' teaching was clear. After the curriculum unit was published, I got a letter signed by all the youth in a junior high class accusing me of not believing the Bible because I had said the text may be a parable. I still can recall reading that letter alone in my office, looking at the youthful signatures on the second page. The battle was about as close to me as it could get. I had wanted the gospel's call to transcend boundaries to invade the horseplay of Sunday night youth group, but, apparently, the youth leader had decided that the real lesson should be about the perceived doctrinal infidelity of seminary professors.

I left this seminary to begin my work at ATS with scores of questions about how seminaries should relate to denominations. What are good and viable relationships for theological schools and their ecclesial communities? ATS has, more than once, dealt with theological schools in the middle of ecclesiastical struggles. In many if not most of these struggles, the seminary was a proxy for other, deeper issues that fueled the conflict. Would theological schools be better off without close and direct connections to church bodies? Will their future, like many church-related colleges, entail a gradual loosening of connections with ecclesial bodies, in order to disentangle educational mission from denominational politics and protect their freedom to study and conduct research?

The Importance of the Theological School-Church Relationship

A meaningful relationship with ecclesial bodies is crucial for theological schools. Michael A. Battle, president of Interdenominational Theological Center, told an ATS audience a few years ago that the church is necessary for the seminary, but the seminary is not necessary for the church. He rushed on to say that the church needs education for its leaders and theological reflection to inform its work, but it doesn't have to have the current version of theological schools to meet that need. The seminary, on the other hand, cannot exist without the church. If no community sends students to seminary, if no denomination or congregation wants to hire any seminary graduates, then most ATS schools have a very limited future. If the church — all of it — were to rise up and say to the seminaries "we don't want you or your graduates," most ATS schools would be like cursed fig trees. They would wither and die. I know this is an arguable hypothesis, but after it is parsed, qualified, and socially located, I think it remains true.

The relationship is also crucial for the church, but the reasons are less obvious. The denomination's organizational existence would not be at stake if it were to cease using theological schools. Church bodies could create temporary, less expensive institutes and training programs for pastors, and they could contract with sympathetic scholars to conduct studies and prepare manuscripts as needed. Some congregations with large memberships are already conducting training programs and workshops in congregational ministry and development. If the relationship were severed and church bodies no longer used seminary graduates, the result would manifest itself slowly and gradually. It would take thirty or forty years before the last seminary graduates retired, so congregations would benefit from the contributions of seminary education long after the schools had closed. Some talented pastors, who would not have the opportunity for a seminary education, would do exceptionally well. Others would struggle and, over time, the effects of a totally nonseminary-educated clergy would begin to show. Like drawing water from a shallow well, the water serves its purpose as long as it lasts, but it will disappear when the drought comes — the very time it may be needed most.

Of course, it is unlikely that either theological schools or ecclesial bodies would decide on a radical split. The real question is about the extent to which schools and churches value their relationships with one another. If the school sees the church as intrusive and obstructive to its educational and research work, it may tolerate the relationship but not value it as important. If the church body sees the school as an unnecessary expense or cannot differentiate seminary-educated clergy from alternatively credentialed pastors, it may tolerate a relationship for historical or fraternal reasons but not see the relationship as significant. The future depends on *both* the church and the school seeing the relationship they share as important and vital, because each understands the contribution that the seminary makes to church and the church to the seminary.

Seminaries make many contributions to the church. In the context of an accrediting visit to a diocesan seminary several years ago, the evaluation committee asked the bishop why he thought it was worth the financial commitment to keep the school operating, with its small enrollment. It would have been less expensive for the diocese to send its priesthood candidates elsewhere. He replied that the seminary served the diocese in many ways in addition to the education of priests and lay professional leaders. Faculty members provided a theological resource for the church in that region, and the church would not be as thoughtful or effective without the contributions they made.

The last fifty years have altered the institutional landscape of many Protestant denominations. A half century ago, these denominations had hospitals and health care centers, and while these institutions continue with the denominational name in their title, the funding of health care has distanced them from the denominations that founded them. A similar pattern exists for children's homes and facilities for the aged. These institutions have become increasingly dependent on public and third-party funding, which translates into decreased connections to the church body. Many denominational colleges and universities have also distanced themselves from their founding organizations. The result of these changes is that denominations no longer have the institutional infrastructure that once channeled ministry efforts and provided expertise and support both to the institutions and the denominations. Theological schools are the only institutions that remain tightly identified with some denominations. Sometimes, the church body uses the institutional resources of the school — recruiting faculty to serve on committees, preach and teach in the congregations, or write for denominational publications — without realizing the institutional support that is necessary for individuals to have the knowledge and time to make these contributions. And then there is the obvious: seminaries educate the leaders that ecclesial communities need. The Auburn Center's most recent study of seminary graduates[1] confirms that schools provide a valuable service for the church. Persons educated for ministry tend to end up in ministry, stay in ministry, and believe that their education provided good preparation for what they are doing. ATS data on entering and graduating students indicate that a higher percentage of students intend to work in congregational ministry at graduation than is true of entering students.

In addition to these instrumental and organizational contributions, seminaries contribute to the lives of congregations and denominations in a more subtle but important way. Theological schools are the primary support the church has for sustaining and renewing its understanding of the meaning and message of the faith. One of the colleagues at the seminary where I taught before joining the ATS staff was a very able New Testament scholar. He left the seminary to become a pastor of a large congregation and, several years later, I visited him. I asked him about the difference between working with the New Testament as a professor and as a pastor. He replied that, as a pastor, there was not time to engage the deeper study of the text that he had enjoyed as a professor. Pastoral work involves study for teaching and preaching, but that work occurs amid all the other tasks that comprise pasto-

---

1. Barbara G. Wheeler, Sharon L. Miller, and Daniel Aleshire, "How Are We Doing? The Effectiveness of Theological Schools as Measured by Vocations and Views of Graduates," *Auburn Reports*, no. 13 (January 2008).

ral leadership. Time for study is limited. He said that pastoral work had many rewards, including teaching the text. However, the kind of study that he had routinely done as a professor was no longer possible. What was true for this talented pastor and professor is, in many ways, true for congregations and denominations. From the modern-day translations of the Bible that are used by most Christians in North America, to the commentaries that pastors use in their sermon preparations, to the occasional study papers that denominations commission — the church depends on theological schools to keep the flame of understanding the religious tradition burning. Schools are not the only place where this happens, but they are a primary place.

The church, and the sense of religious calling and engagement it inculcates, is important to theological schools. Students enroll in theological degree programs because they are interested in the practice of ministry or understanding their faith better or are searching for their own religious identity. All of these are deeply religious reasons and, for most students, congregations or denominations played a crucial role in cultivating this religious sensitivity. Theological schools have no future apart from the religious longings and callings that bring students to classes and the religious questions that invite interest in faculty research. Theological faculty are not just academically interested in their disciplines, they are religiously interested in them. The Auburn Center for the Study of Theological Education has found that faculty members are "deeply and regularly involved in the life of the church at all levels."[2] In a ten-year follow-up survey, the Center found that while fewer faculty members were ordained, they were no less involved in church or religious activities.[3] If the present predicts the future, theological school faculty will continue to reflect religious commitment and involvement.

Why would ecclesial communities conclude that theological

2. Barbara G. Wheeler, "True and False: The First in a Series of Reports from a Study of Theological School Faculty," *Auburn Reports*, no. 4 (January 1996): 16.

3. Barbara G. Wheeler, Sharon L. Miller, and Katarina Schuth, "Signs of the Times: Present and Future Theological Faculty," *Auburn Studies*, no. 10 (February 2005): 17.

schools are no longer valuable? I don't think they will come to that direct conclusion; however, they may conclude that theological schools are not worth their cost, or that with so many pressing needs for declining amounts of money, the schools are not as high a priority as other needs. I believe that a decision to abandon theological schools would resemble a farmer's decision to sell the seed corn because he needed the money. In the short run, it may help; in the long term, the results could be disastrous for the church. As a wise trustee once said to a seminary president, "We must strengthen the school. The seminary is where the future of the church is embodied."[4]

Changes Affecting the Theological School-Church Relationship

Most theological schools were founded by church bodies, primarily for the education of ministers. Seminaries unrelated to a particular denomination were founded for the education of ministers, usually with a particular theological perspective, and most of these nondenominational seminaries have worked very intentionally to cultivate relationships with the denominations with which their students are affiliated. While theological school-church relationships have been strong and continuous since the founding of these schools, the pervasive changes in congregational practices, in denominations, and in the social status of religion in North American culture place new pressures on this long-standing relationship.

Congregational and denominational Christianity is changing. I drive through a county seat town in Ohio on my way to my parents' home. One can see most of downtown from the interstate overpass on the north side of town. Churches dominate the skyline — all of them early twentieth-century stone and brick buildings, most of them with fortress towers. When I have driven by at night, with their towers lighted, these church buildings give the impression of strong and vital institutions. One day, I exited the interstate to look more closely at

---

4. David Tiede, private communication with the author, 2007.

these buildings. As best I could tell from my daytime drive, it appeared that some of these congregations were strong, but others were struggling. I saw one large physical plant with a single pastoral staff member listed on the church marquis, and another church building with what appeared to be an empty upper floor of an education building. By contrast, a newer church at the edge of town had recently built an addition. Elsewhere, I am sure a large Pentecostal congregation is doing well, along with other Evangelical congregations.

If my drive-by analysis is correct, why are the in-town congregations struggling? This city is not very big; it wouldn't take more than ten minutes to get to the old churches from most any part of town. The change is not a function of urban blight or commuting distances. Some religious patterns are growing and some are declining in this Ohio town and in thousands of other communities like it. The relative strength of denominations is changing. The in-town congregations are related to denominations that were dominant when their church buildings were new. Those denominations have experienced decline, and others, many of them nonexistent a century ago, are growing and gaining influence. Some denominations have been declining in membership for forty years, and many theological schools are related to these denominations. Other denominations have been growing, and many theological schools are related to these denominations. The question of church relatedness forces one group of theological schools to come to terms with a loss of vitality and status, and another group of schools to adjust responsibly to being a dominant presence rather than on the sidelines. Theological schools are deeply affected by the status of the religious communities to which they are most closely related. The changing status of religious communities makes it crucial for schools to reassess their ecclesial relationships.

Christianity is changing in other ways, as well.[5] Denominational

---

5. Among the more enduring references about these changes, I would refer readers to Robert Wuthnow, *The Restructuring of American Religion: Society and Faith Since World War II* (Princeton, N.J.: Princeton University Press, 1988) and more recently, Mark Chaves, *Congregations in America* (Cambridge, Mass.: Harvard University Press, 2004).

distinctives and loyalties have dissipated throughout the last half of the twentieth century. Evangelical Protestantism, which in the 1950s would have been the most anti-Catholic Protestant expression, has made common cause with Roman Catholics on issues like opposition to abortion and explored common ground on many historical doctrinal affirmations. A few years ago, *Christianity Today,* a leading Evangelical monthly, published a feature essay about Evangelical interest in the Virgin Mary, and more recently, a Roman Catholic/Evangelical dialogue generated agreement on some historic doctrinal positions. There is still considerable cleavage between these two groups, but it has lessened in the past twenty-five years.[6]

The social status of religion in North American society is changing. In Canada, a quasi-established privilege for religion all but evaporated in the last part of the twentieth century. In the United States, a less established but very evident privilege for religion as a social institution has given way to a more neutral protection of religion as an arena of personal choice. While the United States and Canada are still the most church-attending developed countries in the world (estimates of 25 to 30 percent in the United States who are in attendance at worship any given week — and maybe as much as 10 to 15 percent in Canada — are significantly greater than Great Britain and Western Europe's 5 to 6 percent), the favored status that the culture in both countries extended to religion is eroding.

Phillip Hammond[7] has put forward a very interesting thesis about the "third disestablishment" of American religion. The first, of course, was in the Bill of Rights, when the state churches of the colonies were disallowed in the new United States. While the Bill of Rights disestablished legal privilege for a state church, a cultural privilege was extended to American Protestantism throughout the nineteenth century. The stories in a McGuffey reader, a mainstay of late nineteenth and

6. Bob Allen, "Finding Common Ground with Catholics, Southern Baptist Leaders Question Contraception," *EthicsDaily.com,* 18 October 2006, www.ethics daily.com/article_detail.cfm?AID=8033.

7. Phillip E. Hammond, *Religion and Personal Autonomy: The Third Disestablishment in America* (Columbia, S.C.: University of South Carolina Press, 1992).

early twentieth century public elementary education, demonstrate the religious privilege that was evident in nonreligious, public schools. Laws restricting Sunday commerce continued well past World War II, and tax statutes that excused churches from paying for civic services like police and fire protection were also indicators of this cultural privilege. Hammond argues that the second disestablishment came in the early twentieth century when the privilege that the culture had extended to Protestants was expanded to include Roman Catholics and Jews. Religion was culturally privileged, and the religious range was widened. It became a good thing for the community Thanksgiving service to include a Protestant minister, Jewish rabbi, and Roman Catholic priest. The third disestablishment, in Hammond's view, has been occurring across the past thirty years or so. As religious America has become more diverse, the culture is withdrawing the privilege it had previously granted Protestants, Catholics, and Jews rather than extending it to an ever-growing range of religious sentiments and practices. Religion has shifted from being a societal value to a personal choice. Society protects the individual's right to choose to be religious but does not necessarily claim that religion does any more good for the society than other pro-social activities. Theological schools were founded and have grown to maturity as a resource for a church that enjoyed cultural respect and privilege. Both the schools and the church shared this privilege.

These changes in congregations, parishes, denominations, and the social location of religion mean that all theological schools face challenges, not only in their relationship to ecclesial communities, but also in their educational practices. For Roman Catholics, the continuing decrease in the number of priestly vocations results in more parish work being performed by lay ecclesial ministers. What kind of theological education and formation do these frontline workers need to staff parish life? What kind of formation do candidates for priesthood need as the role of priests is being functionally redefined by their decreasing number? For mainline Protestants, with membership decline resulting in an increasing number of congregations that cannot afford a full-time pastor, alternative patterns for credentialing part-time and bi-vocational clergy are emerging rapidly. Can theological schools continue to operate alternative educational models out of their back pockets as these models become increasingly dominant? How do schools and denominations continue to value theological degrees for those who can obtain them as the number of pastors without them increases? Will there be an increasingly double-tiered understanding of ministry? In the twentieth century, mainline denominations were the most affected by the ecumenical movement. While the movement has not resulted in church union, it has led to the blurring of denominational lines and doctrinal distinctives. What are the implications of that, over time? Evangelical Protestants have emerged as the dominant Protestant presence in the United States and a growing Protestant presence in Canada. Evangelicals have pioneered most of the new-paradigm congregational practices that all Protestants are exploring, and their seminaries have developed more new degree programs, more extension sites, and greater involvement in distance learning programs. Many Evangelical seminaries were founded to protest some aspect of Protestant traditions. Now, the protest has become the dominant expression of Protestantism, and that changes its character and ethos. How will Evangelical schools adjust to their new majority status?

In a previous day, denominations provided theological schools with money, students, and ministry settings for graduates. Seminaries served the denomination by educating leaders, contributing theological expertise in a variety of ways and, sometimes, calling the church to account in one way or another. The church-school relationship was organic and reciprocal. With the very notable exception of a few denominations, these tight relationships are changing. Theological schools need viable and effective relationships with ecclesial communities, and it becomes their responsibility to form the kinds of relationships that will serve new patterns of networking, transdenominational connections, congregational connections, and para-church connections. At times, these partners will approach the seminary, but I think increasingly it will be the seminary's job to initiate and establish relationships with them. Interesting new models of relationship are developing and theological schools have both the creativity and capacity to engage them, invent still others, and provide support and service to the church that will be sorely needed as communities of faith undertake their work in changing contexts and culture.

Education for Future Ministerial Leadership

ATS schools have spent most of the twentieth century developing commonly accepted patterns for their work. If schools carefully attend to the changing fortunes of North American denominations, the future will likely require multiple definitions of good theological education, with very different practices associated with these differing definitions. Most of what was described in the chapters on learning, teaching, and research is the result of the current pattern of theological education. Can multiple patterns of theological education be developed that achieve the same formational learning that cultivates "an aptitude for theological reflection and wisdom pertaining to responsible life in faith"? The answer is yes — but the standard for measuring the value of these new approaches will be that they are as effective at cultivating this aptitude for theological wisdom as the present models are.

Whether future educational patterns are similar or different, they must meet perceived needs for ministerial leadership. In a focus group that ATS convened during a recent project, one pastor of a large-membership church said that when his congregation was looking for staff ministers, it wanted persons who were passionate about faith, gifted in some expression of ministry, and who knew how to multiply that gift in the congregation. Most seminary graduates are not going to be called to large churches, but I am intrigued by his statement of ministerial capacity. In a culture that gives religion a less-esteemed place, the church needs leaders who can passionately make the case for faith, who have the gifts and abilities to lead congregations, and can help those congregations do faith's work in the world. How do current patterns of theological education contribute to these qualities in ministerial leadership? A bishop in another focus group conversation said that pastors need "to be emotionally and spiritually serious human beings. Our congregations are full of anxiety, and if pastors are caught up in this anxiety, they cannot lead." This bishop went on to say that pastors need "to have spiritual maturity . . . [and because] the culture does not appreciate their work, they need to own their religious heritage. We need whole people coming out of seminary, who have their head and heart in the right place."[8]

Another pastor in a focus group commented that seminaries have been very good at educating chaplains for "one-hundred attender" congregations, but that the center of American Christianity is moving away from congregations this size to larger congregations that function very differently. How are current educational strategies preparing students for both kinds of congregations? The National Congregational Survey, conducted in 2001, found that 60 percent of American churches have fewer than one hundred regular participants; 30 percent have between one hundred and three hundred fifty; and 10 percent have more than three hundred fifty.[9] This 10 percent of congregations with attendance over three hundred fifty accounts for more than half of all churchgoers. While the vast majority of congregations and parishes have relatively small memberships, the majority of churchgoers attend larger membership churches. Theological schools need to take seriously this double track: most pastors will serve smaller membership congregations and most churchgoers will attend larger membership congregations and parishes. It would be irresponsible for theological schools to educate students in the pastoral skills that larger congregations and parishes require because most graduates would never have opportunity to use those skills. It would be equally irresponsible for theological schools not to take seriously the larger congregations and their unique educational needs, especially for program staff and ministers.

If theological schools are to serve the church as well in the future as they have in the past, change is going to be required. Fortunately, these institutions are schools, and their institutional capacity and educational

---

8. The Association convened these conversations in fall 2007 and spring 2008 as part of the ATS project on Theological Schools and the Church.

9. Mark Chaves, *Congregations in America*, p. 19.

knowledge provide the necessary resources to make thoughtful and appropriate changes. They have changed in the past, and are capable of changing in the future. Institutions do not change quickly, and they don't change radically at any one moment. But they do change over time and the accrual of that change can be dramatic. One of the strengths of theological schools, as institutions, is that they not only change but can do so in a way that preserves the best of the heritage from which they have come. Congregations and denominations change more quickly than institutional theological schools do. Schools almost always change in response to the church; the church almost never changes in response to affiliated theological schools. This makes it incumbent on the schools to track change, discriminate the substantive movement and direction of change from ephemeral enticements along the way, and make the changes they need to make to serve the future.

Academy: Theological Schools and Higher Education

Most ATS schools began as "abbeys," in David Tiede's image. Some even looked like abbeys — built in semirural environments in retreat-like settings. As the twentieth century progressed, theological schools became more interested in developing relationships and recognition in the broader world of higher education. ATS began as a conference of theological schools in 1918. However, following efforts in medicine to make medical practice more scientific by accrediting medical schools, efforts in law to make legal education more academic through law school accreditation, and the growth of regional accreditation in the United States, the conference voted in 1936 to adopt the first standards of accrediting for theological schools. Although substantially different from the current standards, they clearly were an effort to increase higher education expectations and define theological education as post-baccalaureate education. The "abbey" schools began to understand themselves more as academic institutions and to follow the conventions of the broader world of higher education.

ATS member schools grant graduate, professional degrees. Eighty percent of the freestanding schools in the United States are accredited by one of six regional accrediting agencies in addition to ATS. Many have joint degree programs with colleges or universities, most accept credits from other higher education institutions, and most other higher education institutions accept credits from ATS schools. The Commission on Accrediting of ATS is recognized both by the Council on Higher Education Accreditation and the U.S. Department of Education for the accreditation of post-baccalaureate theological education. In every way that one would determine if a school is a higher education institution in the United States or Canada, ATS member schools meet the determination.

Higher education in North America is diverse, highly valued, and carries a worldwide reputation. It includes publicly funded universities, church-related and Christian colleges and universities, and other private institutions. Some schools are comprehensive research universities, others are small colleges, some are highly selective in admissions, others have open admissions policies, some are liberal arts colleges, still others are community colleges or technical institutes, and others, like ATS schools, are special-purpose institutions. The diversity of educational mission is expansive. Higher education in North America has been highly valued, both by citizens in the United States and Canada, and by persons and institutions outside North America. The G-8 countries together enroll two-thirds of all students studying outside their own countries, and the United States enrolls 22 percent of the international students enrolled by all G-8 countries. Eleven percent of all higher education students in Canada are from other countries.[10] ATS schools, in many ways, share in this esteem. They have a high percentage of international students, and many of them serve as centers of learning for the worldwide ecclesial families with which they are associated.

Along with its status and generally high esteem, and among many

10. D. C. Miller, A. Sen, and L. B. Malley, *Comparative Indicators of Education in the United States and Other G-8 Countries: 2006*, NCES 2007-2006 (Washington, D.C.: National Center for Education Statistics, Institute of Education Sciences, U.S. Department of Education, August 2007), www.nces.ed.gov/pubs2007/2007006_1.pdf.

evidences of success, higher education in the United States is facing several challenges. A 2006 report of a Commission appointed by the U.S. Secretary of Education (the Spellings Commission) characterized U.S. higher education as "an enterprise that has yet to address the fundamental issues of how academic programs and institutions must be transformed to serve the changing educational needs of a knowledge economy. It has yet to successfully confront the impact of globalization, rapidly evolving technologies, an increasingly diverse and aging population, and an evolving marketplace characterized by new needs and new paradigms."[11] While the report affirms the unique gifts of American higher education, the Commission, often reflecting the sentiment of business and other national leaders, perceives widespread problems. The report will likely go the way of other reports of federal agencies that stir debate, raise anxiety, and provide leverage for bureaucratic maneuvering, but in the end, do not effect significant change. I take exception to many of the fundamental assumptions in the Spellings Commission report, but it raises three issues that provide a lens for examining theological schools as higher education institutions: affordability, access, and accountability.

Affordability

Higher education can be very inexpensive at a publicly funded community college or four-year institution, or very expensive at some private colleges and universities. In fall 2007, George Washington University made the news as the first U.S. school whose tuition, room, and board fees exceeded fifty thousand dollars per year. After scholarships and other forms of support, it is not clear how many students will actually pay that amount, but some will. The Spellings Commission recommended that "Policymakers and higher education leaders should develop, at the institutional level, new and innovative means to con-

---

11. U.S. Department of Education, *A Test of Leadership: Charting the Future of U.S. Higher Education* (Washington, D.C., 2006), http://www.ed.gov/about/bdscomm/list/hiedfuture/reports/final-report.pdf.

trol costs, improve productivity, and increase the supply of higher education."[12] The language of this statement is interesting. "Productivity improvements" and "increasing supply" are not terms that have been associated with higher education's ongoing struggle to meet costs and remain affordable. While they describe common strategies for business in a free-market economy, this language could not be further removed from the educational purposes of eighteenth- and nineteenth-century colleges, with their concern for the cultivation of character and education of persons for responsible citizenship. The language of the report suggests that higher education has been reconceptualized as a commodity: it is a product that has a price tag on it, and the social goal is to provide the best-value educational product for the least amount of tuition and public money. The Commission's concern is that higher education has become too expensive to be afforded by the percentage of the population that need higher education if the United States is to stay competitive as a knowledge-based economy in a global marketplace.

Funding for many schools is problematic. The Spellings Commission does not have theological education in view, and its strategies for reducing costs convey a perception that higher education is more expensive than it needs to be. The Commission appears to think that even if schools are not getting rich while students and their families struggle with tuition, they are not doing enough to curtail costs. I am not sure how true this is in higher education but I know that it is not the case with theological schools. ATS statistics on institutional finance suggest that as many as 20 percent of theological schools in North America are financially stressed. (Stress is defined here as schools that have had operating deficits three out of the last five years, or possess expendable assets that would carry them for fewer than three months if all forms of income stopped.) The schools show the strain of financing theological education. For the most part, theological schools cannot operate less expensively than they do. Salaries are the major cost in a seminary budget, and compensation in theological schools is generally lower than compensation in other higher educa-

12. U.S. Department of Education, *A Test of Leadership.*

tion institutions with similar levels of degree programs. Because most theological schools are not in competition with each other, they are not in the facilities and program competition that some undergraduate schools are in, with the attendant escalation of costs. ATS schools tend to function as cost-effectively as small institutions can, and are succeeding in keeping costs low.

While theological schools have worked to keep costs low, and many are themselves financially stressed, the cost of theological education is a growing burden for students in the United States. In an earlier era, abundant denominational funding made theological education very inexpensive for students. Some denominations, like the Southern Baptist Convention, the Church of the Nazarene, and others, continue to subsidize their theological schools at a significant level, which keeps tuition very low. Other ATS schools have sufficient endowments to provide scholarships that cover virtually all the costs of tuition. Annual tuition for basic ministerial degrees is not high, compared to tuition for other post-baccalaureate programs. In 2006-07, it averaged twelve thousand dollars in the United States and about six thousand dollars in Canada (the result of provincial grants to many Canadian schools that provide direct support to the school but are attended with tuition price controls). Students, however, bear about one-third of the cost of their theological degree program.[13] The remaining two-thirds of needed revenue is derived from endowment, gifts from religious organizations, and gifts from individuals.[14]

The overall cost of attending theological schools, however, is greater than tuition. It includes living and other expenses, and the rising cost is evidenced in growing levels of educational debt. In a 2007 survey of more than five thousand graduates of ATS schools, 47 percent of respondents reported that they had incurred no educational debt upon graduation, and 11 percent said they were graduating with less than ten

13. *Graduating Student Questionnaire: 2006-2007 Profile of Participants* (Pittsburgh: The Association of Theological Schools in the United States and Canada, 2007).

14. *2006-2007 Annual Data Tables,* www.ats.edu/SiteCollectionDocuments/AnnualDataTables/2006-07AnnualDataTables.pdf.

thousand dollars of seminary educational debt. Thus, the news is good for almost 60 percent of the graduates. However, 23 percent reported that they had incurred between ten and thirty thousand dollars of educational debt, and 19 percent said that they were graduating with debt greater than thirty thousand dollars. Repayment of debt greater than thirty thousand dollars likely will be difficult if a graduate's income is limited to the average salary for entry-level ministry positions.

Concerns about the cost of theological education are not so much concerns about the absolute dollar expenditure as they are concerns about whether graduate theological education is worth the cost. This is a different issue than that expressed in the Commission's report. There, the argument is made that higher education is vital to the national well-being and, therefore, must be widely affordable for the government, students, and their families. In theological education, the talk about cost often turns to discussion about whether graduate, professional theological education is worth it, not how to keep it affordable. Is the work that these schools do worth the price tag? If theological education is a commodity to be produced at the least expense for the most recipients, then the question is legitimate. If the goal, however, is the preparation of religious leaders who are deeply formed in an understanding of faith, who can guide congregations in a culture that is less than convinced that religion is a cultural asset, who can lead in the context of significant change in congregational practice, and who both know the tradition and can teach it to the increasing percentage of people who do not know the tradition or understand it, then theological education is not a commodity. Seminaries are founded when religious expressions are growing, and their greatest need might be when those expressions are struggling. The question about cost is really a question about value. Christianity is better funded in North America than anywhere else in the world. Funds are always tight, of course, but they are available. If seminaries fail in the future because of inadequate financing, it won't be because there is not enough money available. It will be because there is an inadequate commitment to the essential contribution that theological schools make to the Christian project and religious leadership.

Access

The Spellings Commission concluded that too few people attend college or university, and attribute this failure to inadequate high school preparation, achievement gaps disproportionately affecting low income and racial/ethnic students, inadequate capacity of programs designed for students over twenty-four years of age (40 percent of all postsecondary students in the United States), lack of or confusing information about higher education opportunities, and the lingering results of affordability issues. Theological schools, once again, demonstrate that they are part of higher education on issues related to access, but not in quite the same way. Access is a serious concern for theological schools, and I want to address two issues related to it. The first is the combination of location of theological schools, older students, and residency requirements of the ATS accrediting standards. The second is the percentage of racial/ethnic students in ATS schools.

Theological schools, since their earliest expressions in the United States and Canada, have focused theological education on the formational interaction of students and teachers. As noted earlier in this essay, graduates rate their interaction with faculty as one of the most influential aspects of their seminary experience, and rate their interaction with other students almost as high. Theological schools provide learning in community. Theological learning is not just about religious ideas; it is about religious ideas that lead to religious commitment and human engagement. It is about skills and abilities that occur in human community, like preaching, pastoral care, and administration. One of the longest traditions and deepest commitments in theological education is that teachers and learners should study together over time. This practice is formalized in the ATS accrediting standards that require each master's degree to include at least one year of residential study on the primary campus of the school granting the degree. "Residence" does not necessarily mean living on campus; it is generally interpreted to mean that students take the equivalent of a full year of courses on the campus. These courses may be offered in short, intensive blocks of time, and students may take them over many years, but they add up to the equivalent of one full-time year's work.

The residency requirement functioned without much concern when most students were young and single, and tuition was very low or nonexistent. These students could put most of their possessions in the car and drive to the seminary of their denomination, wherever it was located. However, something began to happen forty years ago. Older students, many married and with children, began seeking seminary education. A portion of this over-thirty group was women who had not pursued theological education because most mainline Protestant denominations had not previously ordained women. With the opportunity to serve in pastoral ministry, women began to come to seminary. Other reasons led other students over thirty to seek seminary education. Older students cannot move as easily as younger students. They have children in school and much greater income needs than single students. If married, they are often dependent on their spouse's income for support during seminary, and while the student could move, the spouse cannot and still provide sufficient family income.

If seminaries were evenly located throughout North America, residency would not pose a problem for older students. However, that is not the case. Schools are located where they are for historical reasons, not for the current distribution of the population. Two-thirds of all schools in the United States and Canada are located in the eastern third of the two nations. In 1990, Orlando, Charlotte, Phoenix, Miami, Houston, San Diego, Portland, and Seattle had either one or no ATS accredited school. Even within some denominations, the seminaries are not distributed so that they are convenient to the current population centers of the denomination. For example, the seminaries funded by the Southern Baptist Convention, the largest Protestant denomination in the United States, are located in southern Louisiana, eastern North Carolina, and Louisville — effectively on the far borders of the denominational population center in the Southeast. The other three schools are located in Texas, Missouri, and California. Only the Texas school is located in a heavily Southern Baptist population area.

The residency requirement, age of students, and location of the schools combine to make access an issue. Students who would like to study can't because family or financial issues make it impractical for them to move. Schools have addressed the access issue by developing extension sites (professor and students in a classroom away from the main campus). Since 1996, they have developed distance learning programs (computer-assisted instruction where students are working online with the professor and other students) complemented with intensive courses on campus. Each of these accommodations, however, modifies the educational conviction that students and faculty should be physically in the same place for theological study. There are many who would like theological schools to eliminate the residency requirement. Nothing would increase access more dramatically. Many master's degrees and even some Ph.D.s offered by regionally accredited institutions can be earned by distance learning programs that require no residential study. Why not theological education? If more theological education were available online, more part-time and bi-vocational clergy could earn degrees from ATS schools. Wouldn't that be preferable to the often ad hoc structures and teaching of alternative credentialing programs? Theological schools were invented, for the most part, to educate religious leadership. As more of that leadership in many denominations are not able to attend seminary in the traditional way, should theological schools maximize access by eliminating the expectation of theological study in the context of residential classes, where students and faculty interact in formative ways? Or, should they hold on to residential study because it is the primary way in which the formational learning has been proven effective?

Access is also an issue for some racial/ethnic minority students. ATS schools offer degree programs that require students to have bachelor's degrees to be admitted. The Spellings Commission cited the following data as the basis for its concern about access to American higher education. By age twenty-nine (because students take longer to complete baccalaureate degrees, it is important to increase the age by which determination is made about major trends in degree completion), 34 percent of whites have obtained a bachelor's degree, 17 percent of African Americans, and 11 percent of Latinos/Hispanics. The largest issue of access to ATS schools for racial/ethnic students is the differential rate of baccalaureate completion.[15]

There are two ways to consider the enrollment of racial/ethnic students in ATS schools to determine problems related to access. The first is by comparing enrollments in theological schools to enrollments in similar programs in higher education. The second is to compare percentages of racial/ethnic enrollment to percentages in the general population. As to the first, ATS enrollments of racial/ethnic students approximate enrollments in U.S. graduate and first professional degree programs (the national category that most closely parallels ATS degree programs). In 2005, ATS schools in the United States had a higher percentage of African American students (12.2 percent for ATS schools compared to 10.3 percent in U.S. graduate and professional degree programs), a lower percentage of Hispanic/Latino students (4.1 percent in ATS schools compared to 5.9 percent for the United States), and similar percentages of Asian students (6.2 percent in ATS schools, 6.5 percent in U.S.) and native peoples (.3 percent for ATS and .5 percent for U.S.). As to the second method of comparison, ATS schools in the U.S. enroll African Americans at about the same percentage as their presence in the population (12.2 percent of the ATS school enrollment, and 12.8 percent of the population); Asians at a higher percentage than their proportion of the population (6.2 percent of ATS enrollment and 4.3 percent of U.S. population); and Hispanic/Latino students at a dramatically lower percentage than in the general population (4.1 percent of the ATS enrollment and 14.4 percent of the population).

These data suggest that Hispanics have special problems with access to theological education. Three issues are likely most responsible for the underrepresentation of Hispanic/Latino students in theological schools. The first is the baccalaureate requirement for admission. The Hispanic/Latino community has the lowest percentage of baccalaureate

---

15. These data are quoted in the report of the Spellings Commission, which drew them from Nicole Stoops, *Educational Attainment in the United States: 2003*. Current Population Reports P20-550. (Washington, D.C.: U.S. Census Bureau, 2004).

degree holders of any racial/ethnic group in the United States. Many ATS schools with special programs for Hispanic students have reported that their biggest recruiting problem is the baccalaureate requirement. A second issue is the relatively large percentage of Hispanics/Latinos/Latinas who are Roman Catholic or Pentecostal. Roman Catholics have a low percentage of participation in theological schools (as determined by the ratio of total membership in the U.S. church to Roman Catholics enrolled in ATS schools), and Pentecostals do not require graduate degrees for ordination or ministerial service. A third reason is language. Spanish is the first language for many Hispanics/Latinos/, and English is second. The technical terms associated with advanced studies in the theological disciplines can be difficult for English speakers, let alone persons who speak English as a second language.[16]

Access is of critical importance for theological schools. They cannot serve the educational needs of communities of faith if the persons those communities need as leaders cannot attend a theological school. What strategies would increase access? If ATS schools began offering theological education at both the bachelor's and master's degree levels, that would create access for many. It would be a major change in the way theological degrees have been understood since the 1930s in the United States and Canada and would run contrary to trends in other areas of higher education, such as secondary teacher education, in which baccalaureate programs are shifting toward master's level programs in many colleges and universities. ATS could remove the residency requirement, which would also increase access. Removing this requirement, however, could constitute a significant threat to the quality of formational learning. There may be patterns of sustained peer and mentor relationships that address the formational goal of residency, but such programs would need to be thoughtfully developed and carefully administered. ATS schools have worked hard to increase the enrollment of racial/ethnic students. However, the real access solu-

16. Kenneth Davis and Edwin Hernandez have conducted a major study of Hispanics in theological education. See *Reconstructing the Sacred Tower: Challenge and Promise of Latino/a Theological Education* (Princeton, N.J.: Hispanic Theological Initiative Series vol. 3, 2005).

tion may be to provide the kind of education that racial/ethnic students most need to serve in the settings where they are most likely to minister.

Accountability

The Spellings Commission worries a great deal about accountability and transparency in higher education institutions. If you have known any high school seniors who have been trying to make decisions about colleges or universities recently, you know how much mail they have received and how frustrated their parents can be not knowing how much college is going to cost until offers of admission and financial aid are made. Higher education is hard to figure out at times, and it is especially hard to compare one school to another. In a free market economy, however, there is a presumption that comparative information on higher education should be available like it is on consumer products at the grocery store. The presumption is not unreasonable, but it is also laden with a particular philosophy of education. It assumes that at least subgroups of schools are trying to accomplish the same thing educationally, that what they are trying to accomplish can be measured, and that it can be measured with enough accuracy to make meaningful comparisons across schools. This is a huge and, I think, untenable assumption. Counterarguments to all these points are many, and debate in the higher education world is relatively intense about what kind of accountability higher education should have and what kind of transparency is most valuable. The Commission recommended that "To meet the challenges of the twenty-first century, higher education must change from a system primarily based on reputation to one based on performance."[17]

This is not so much a recommendation for the future as it is affirmation of a change that is already under way in higher education. The definition of the good school is changing. If you were to ask the question, "What makes Harvard a great school?" most people would re-

17. U.S. Department of Education, *A Test of Leadership.*

spond that it has a twenty billion dollar endowment, which makes it possible for the university to have a world-class faculty, the facilities and program resources it needs to conduct its educational and research programs, and the ability to attract the most academically gifted students. But that is an old response based on reputation. The newer response, affirmed by the Commission's report, is that Harvard is a great school if its students have learned what was intended for them to learn and become the kind of leaders in society that their learning has prepared them to be. It is a great school if Harvard's faculty have done cutting-edge research that advances knowledge and human understanding, and if its centers and schools have contributed creative solutions to problems in government, medicine, divinity, law, business, and education. The new answer is that educational "goodness" is tied to performance, not to resources or reputation.

Theological education differs from higher education in some ways on this debate. Most seminary students are not looking for theological schools in the way that high school seniors are looking for a college or university to attend. If they are United Methodist, they are looking for either a United Methodist school or one approved by the University Senate of the United Methodist Church. If they are Roman Catholic priesthood candidates, they are looking at only the schools that their sending bishop has authorized. If they are Church of the Nazarene, and want to attend the denominational seminary, there is only one choice, as is the case for many denominations. Theological schools do not operate in an open market fashion. Students choose schools primarily for two reasons: theological position and geographical location. Academic reputations are valued, but the primary sources of information about these reputations are pastors and graduates. Every once in a while, ATS receives a question about which theological schools are most highly ranked. No one, including ATS, ranks theological schools. There is no metric for comparing a small, Roman Catholic diocesan seminary with a large, nondenominational Evangelical seminary with a mid-sized mainline Protestant school. Theological schools are simply not competitive with one another in the ways that law or medical schools are.

Nor is there a common measure of educational success that could compare educational effectiveness across all of these different schools. Different ecclesial communities have different expectations about outcomes, and while there is some overlap, there is considerable variation. In the 1970s, ATS undertook the development of the Readiness for Ministry instruments (now Profiles of Ministry) in an effort to develop a common assessment of educational effectiveness. While the instrument continues to be used widely with considerable educational value, it became clear in the developmental phase that the initial goal of a common instrument to assess educational effectiveness across all schools could not be attained. The Commission on Accrediting of ATS expects schools to be able to identify the learning goals of their degree programs and provide evidence regarding the extent to which students have attained those goals. This information, however, is not comparative because different schools have different emphases in their otherwise common educational goals.

Transparency has an ethical dimension, and ATS schools relate ethically and appropriately to their constituencies. ATS publishes a summary of institutional characteristics across all ATS schools. It includes the annual tuition for the Master of Divinity and Doctor of Ministry programs, as well as other data that make comparisons across schools on institutional demographic data. There is no similar listing for colleges or universities in the United States. ATS schools could, and perhaps should, identify the percentage of students who complete degree programs, how long it takes students to finish their programs of study, how many graduates obtain positions related to their degree programs and vocational intent, and how long it takes them to find these positions. These data could increase transparency in useful ways for students.

Theological schools have learned and benefited from the academy. They are better because they have adopted many of the conventions of higher education in North America. However, those conventions and practices are strategies that have been adopted over years, and a school is the kind of institution that is continually evaluating its strategies. If they are not working well, or are no longer needed, they should be abandoned. Communities of faith need intellectually substantive support, but the particular conventions of higher education at a particular point in time are not synonymous with intellectual excellence. For example, the criteria for faculty tenure and promotion typically favor peer-reviewed technical writing over writing for denominational or lay audiences. No intellectual reason dictates this distinction; it is a function of current conventions in higher education. It serves some disciplines very well but may not be ideal for theological education. Higher education accreditation typically favors faculty with research doctorates over faculty with professional doctorates or with exceptional professional experience and no doctorate. While this convention generally serves higher education, it may impede some of the practice-based intellectual work of theological schools. The growth and development of theological schools as higher education institutions has advanced their work and helped to rescue schools from some of the problems associated with their earlier years as abbeys of the church. Educational strategies are means to goals, but they are not the goal.

The next twenty-five years in theological education will result in a great deal more change than the previous twenty-five have. Thomas Friedman, in his recent, popular book, *The World Is Flat,* talks about how major factors have come together to precipitate the changes he describes.[18] Transformation comes about as many factors come into alignment, and theological education will change because factors in American Christianity and American higher education have coalesced in particular ways at a particular time. Even if the world is not flat, it is clear that the world in which theological schools are embedded has changed, is changing, and likely will continue to change.

18. Thomas L. Friedman, *The World Is Flat: A Brief History of the Twenty-first Century* (New York: Farrar, Straus, and Giroux, 2005).

Apostolate: Theological Schools and the Christian Movement

How will theological schools serve the future of the Christian movement? Theological schools grew into their present forms when Christianity was a culturally established and privileged institution in North America. The Christian story was widely known and served as cultural anchor in many ways. How do these schools serve the future when Christianity is less central to North American cultural identity? When the Christian story is generally known in a society, and the church's status and value is presumed, theological schools need to provide intellectual ballast, critique popular religion, and serve as a reforming movement to the church's thinking. Is the role of the school the same when the Christian story and the church's status are more marginal?

David Tiede's image of the school as apostolate suggests that the seminary becomes an advocate for the Christian movement in a different way than in the past. This involves a change not so much in its work as in basic orientation. It would mean, for example, that instead of complaining that students arrive at seminary knowing too little of the Christian story, the faculty accepts this reality and uses its pedagogical skill to enhance the catechetical dimension of the school's educational mission. Instead of assuming that its fundamental job is prophetic witness to social and churchly powers (the social is no longer listening and the churchly no longer has much power), schools understand the increasing priestly side of their work — supporting the work of stressed communities of faith and working to sustain the Christian story as it moves through a very different cultural future in North America. It educates religious leaders to know how to work in congregations and other settings at a time when the culture assigns limited prestige to their work or the institutions they serve.

This apostolic dimension will require a more rabbinic model of Christian ministry. No religion has existed over more millennia in culturally estranged settings than Judaism. Jewish congregational life and rabbinic work have developed over this long period of time in ways that sustain the tradition with limited cultural support and frequent cultural opposition. I don't think the future holds any of the prejudice and persecution for Christians that Jews have experienced, but I do think that Christianity in North America will be decreasingly valued by the culture as a social institution that is integral to social well-being. Christianity will need to find resources internal to the tradition to replace resources that were external but nevertheless contributed to its success in North American culture.

The Christian religion is alive and well, even prospering in North America, but it is prospering most dramatically in those communities that have learned to live without cultural blessing and at times with cultural disdain, like Pentecostals. Christianity has been a vibrant and lively part of North American life, and in the future, it will be lively and vital, as well. Theological schools can contribute to the apostolic mission of the church in several ways. The first is by educating students and the church for the racially changed world that North America is becoming. The second is by engaging constructively with global Christianity. A third is by helping the church address the growing presence of world religions in North America, and finally, by doing what schools can most uniquely do: bear public witness within academic settings.

Theological schools serve the apostolic mission of the church as they educate an increasing percentage of racial/ethnic students and expand the cultural horizon of white students. Sometime in this century, "white" will cease to be the majority race. Ministry in the future in North America will occur in a racially changed world. Theological schools serve the Christian movement as they create the institutional practices that will increase their pedagogical capacity to educate students for the racial/ethnic and multicultural settings as a historic racial majority gives way to racial pluralism. The Christian movement needs theological guidance, ministerial skill, sociological analysis, and congregational resources as it moves through these changes.

Christianity is changing globally. Philip Jenkins has documented the way in which and extent to which Christianity is changing in its worldwide scope.[19] While Christianity is stable or declining in the

19. Philip Jenkins, *The Next Christendom: The Coming of Global Christianity* (Oxford: Oxford University Press, 2002).

Global North, it is growing fast in the Global South. Consider Roman Catholics, for example. The number of Roman Catholics is predicted to grow by large percentages in Latin America and Africa while it will grow by a smaller percentage in North America and decline in Europe. The geographic center of Christianity has historically migrated. In its earliest years, it moved from Jerusalem to Asia Minor and then Rome. It spread from Rome to all of Europe, and from Europe to North and South America. Of course, Christianity also moved east to India and China, and from its earliest years, had a presence in northern Africa. In the mid-twentieth century, the center of the Christian movement was in Europe and North America. In the twenty-first century, the center of Christian growth and numeric dominance will be the Global South. Because religion is always shaped by the culture in which it emerges, Christianity takes on different forms in these areas. In the Global South, Christianity is "far more enthusiastic, much more centrally concerned with the immediate workings of the supernatural, through prophecy, visions, ecstatic utterances, and healing."[20] This is only one description of many ways in which Christianity varies by region. Reformed Protestantism doesn't look the same in Ghana as it does in New York — and the difference is due, in part, to the shape of the culture in both Ghana and New York.

While Christianity changes in discernable ways as it moves into different cultures, it has yet to perfect itself. Christianity showed flaws in Christendom Europe; it showed flaws in North America, and it will reveal flaws in the Global South. Christianity has a way of correcting some things as it moves (like the problems of the state churches in Europe when it came to North America), but it creates new problems (like the ease with which Christians in North America accepted and even endorsed the cultural subjugation of native peoples). Christianity will not perfect itself in the areas of the world where it is growing the fastest. ATS schools serve the future of the church as they transcend cultural and religious practice barriers both to learn from new Christian movements and to teach them. Christians in the North and West

20. Jenkins, *The Next Christendom*, p. 108.

have learned some things from their exuberant years that could be good lessons for churches in the South and East. Some Christian communities in the South and East live with considerable threat, and the developed world can learn from people for whom religious freedom is a distant hope. I was in a meeting with one hundred seminary presidents from South America, the Middle East, Africa, and Asia. One mentioned that teachers routinely teach away from windows because of random gunfire aimed at the seminary. Christianity learns some things as it lives in a culture. Christians in the West have learned from nineteenth-century missionary efforts about how easily cultural values can mask as Christian values, and they can help Christians in the global South critically examine the cultural conventions of their Christianity. Theological schools may be the ideal partners for this exchange of learning and teaching. Among other things, ATS schools need to pay far more attention to scholarship from the global South and East. North American schools represent centers of scholarship and library resources that need to be shared with the majority world. Many ATS schools are in partner-school relationships with educational institutions in these areas, and more should be developed. Thoughtful programs of faculty and student exchange would enlarge the worldview of ATS schools and benefit other schools as well.

Theological schools exercise apostolic service to Christianity in North America by addressing the growth of religious communities other than the Christian and Jewish faiths with which they have been most closely identified. The increasing number of adherents to other world religions in North America will invariably affect the practice of Christian ministry. Ministers and priests will need to be better informed about the commitments and practices of these religious communities; they will need to expand their own theology with a theology of world religions; and they will need to be able to minister in the contexts of inter-religious interaction and engagement in the settings where they will serve. Religion has been both a uniting and divisive factor, and ATS schools will need to identify those practices that the majority religion in North America should undertake to ensure religion's positive contribution as the continent experiences the increasing presence and cultural power of other faiths.[21] These practices will differ by ecclesial community because theologies of world religions will vary markedly in those communities. One creative response has been undertaken by Hartford Seminary, with its long tradition of study on Muslim-Christian relations. Recently, the school developed a program in which imams are studying with Christian ministers. The richness of the educational experience is increased because the discussion about these two religions is not theoretical and philosophical, but personal and confessional, as these students leave class to lead prayer and worship in their respective communities. This example is one of many things schools could do to provide leadership in an area rich with opportunity and riddled with threat.

Finally, theological schools participate in the apostolic mission of the church as they do what schools are uniquely equipped to do: speak to the broader and frequently more secular academic world. Many divinity schools are located in well-known and widely influential research universities. ATS undertook a project on the public character of theological schools a decade ago, and found that universities value the presence of divinity schools and look to them for guidance on moral and ethical issues, as well as the role of religion in society. Denominations and congregations have very limited access to the academic world, but theological schools have a direct, and sometimes very welcome, access. Religion has many public faces, and while its academic face is more interior and less headline-oriented than some others, it may be among the most powerful forms of public presence. Colleges and universities are influential environments that touch almost every sector of civic life. Surveys of students have shown an increasing interest in religion and spirituality, and while congregations and campus-based ministries are effectively reaching them, theological schools can advance religion's nuanced and technical voice to the academic community. Theological schools certainly have a public role that is larger

---

21. Similar language was first used in a draft of the ATS work plan and is employed, with modifications, here.

than the academic community, but they have a unique opportunity within the academic world.

Theological schools continue to serve as abbeys within very particular religious communities, even as those communities are experiencing significant, if not traumatic change. They function as academies — special-purpose higher education institutions — at a time when higher education is both highly revered and severely critiqued. If they have not yet done so, they need to learn to be apostolates, providing the intellectual and educational support that the Christian project will require as it moves into a new era in North America and blossoms with new energy elsewhere in the world. I have argued all along that schools have value because they have the institutional capacity and educational skill to serve the current context and to change in order to serve new and different contexts. Schools don't like to change and will avoid it when they can. The future will present the need for change that schools will not be able to avoid, and because they are *schools*, they won't.

The Work of Theological Schools
and the Future of Communities of Faith

As part of a planning process a few years ago, ATS conducted discussions with presidents and deans across the Association. Careful notes of the discussions were taken and as I read them, one comment leaped out at me: "Is there value to the church in having *educated* clergy?" Theological education takes many forms: institutes and congregation-based programs, training programs for part-time and bi-vocational clergy, undergraduate programs in ministry, and the post-graduate, professional education conducted by ATS schools. What is the value of *seminary-educated* religious leaders? As the first decade of this century is nearing its end, it costs about one hundred thousand dollars per student for theological schools to provide a three-year M. Div. education. Compared to other forms of graduate professional education, like medicine and law, the cost of a theological degree is relatively low. But to the world of forever-strained finances in North American Christianity, it's hardly pocket change. What good does this education do?

The Work of Theological Schools

I conclude this essay where I began in chapter one. The work of theological schools, when done wisely and well, provides a unique and invaluable gift to communities of faith.

Theological schools, first of all, are an indispensable resource for learning for religious vocation. This vocation flourishes when people understand the Christian story, understand human frailty and faithful responses to it, comprehend the gospel's vision of wholeness for individuals and communities, and know how to lead so as to increase human healing, personal righteousness, and social justice. The learning that cultivates these qualities grows out of disciplined study of texts and traditions, critical reflection on experience, and personal engagement in community. It requires contexts that provide sustained, integrated, formational education — exactly the contexts that theological schools cultivate. The educational settings of theological schools maximize the potential for students to learn complex lessons well and, in the context of learning those lessons, to be formed intellectually, spiritually, and morally. Theological schools incubate the kind of theological understanding that contributes to responsible life in faith and faithful leadership of religious communities.

The Christian tradition is a teaching tradition, and theological schools are ideal settings for teaching. As cultural awareness of the Christian story dims, the Christian project needs centers of study that sustain the story in historically informed and intellectually lively ways. It needs teachers who have learned the story deeply and intimately, who understand how the story critiques the culture and how culture critiques that story, and who are capable of teaching students in seminaries and adults in congregations and parishes. As centers of teaching, theological schools provide a critical resource to communities of faith.

Theological schools are also centers of research, and when that research is done with intellectual sophistication and appropriate attention to the needs of communities of faith, it helps the church remember the past, evaluate the present, envision the future, and live faithfully in relationship to all three. Each era of the Christian tradition must identify the truest understanding of the long tradition, the most intellectually faithful Christian witness, and the most honest engagement of the culture and church. Theological schools provide an ideal setting for this kind of intellectual work. Theological research takes time, library resources, the stimulation and methodological correction of other researchers, the questions that students raise, and an informed understanding of a wide range of issues. Schools provide support for all of these elements. While other settings support intellectual work, schools comprise one of the best possible settings for theological research. As centers of faithful intellectual inquiry, schools support the efforts of faith communities to locate the underpinnings of their beliefs in the intellectual idiom of their time and culture.

Theological schools generate more than the sum of learning, teaching, and research. When learning for religious vocation, teaching ministers and church members, and theological research are done in close connection with each other, over time, in communities of common interest, the result is fundamentally different than if these activities are done separately. Each is enhanced when performed in the context of the others, and a school provides a singular context that brings them together in both expectation and practice.

Theological schools are worth the money. The education they provide is worth the effort. The contribution they make to communities of faith is worth the investment. In an era when new seminary students know less of the Christian tradition than previous generations knew, when North American culture is less aware of the Christian story than it has ever been, and when the work of ministry has become more complex and less predictable, the educational response cannot be to lower expectations. While educational efforts need to be broadened to include persons who enter ministry without baccalaureate degrees or without seminary education, broadening alternative educational opportunities cannot mean lowering expectations for theological learning. In an era like this one, theological learning at every level needs to be enhanced, and the work of theological schools becomes even more important. Communities of faith need pastors, ministers, priests, and theologically educated lay leaders who have learned the lessons these schools teach. The Christian message calls for both the highest and broadest patterns of theological learning.

Theological Schools and the Future

The King James Bible that my parents gave me in childhood was difficult to understand. The elegant but incomprehensible language of many passages left me baffled about their meaning. One such passage was from the Sermon on the Mount: "Ye are the salt of the earth; but if the salt have lost its savour, wherewith shall it be salted? It is therefore good for nothing. . . ." One of the few items in my mother's kitchen when I was growing up that remains a staple today is a round, blue box of Morton's salt. While other items in the pantry grew old and stale, the salt never did. The verse didn't make sense to me. How could salt lose its saltiness? Maybe salt functioned differently in biblical times than it did in central Ohio in the 1950s! The verse, I eventually learned, is not about the science of salt; it is a metaphor. If the only purpose that salt serves is to season and preserve food, then losing that capacity renders it good for nothing.

Several years ago, the Association was working on its mission statement. The discussions were clear about the part that deals with "the improvement and enhancement of theological schools." What was not clear at first, but became so upon reflection, is that improvement and enhancement are not enough. Theological schools could be good, but tragically, they could be good for nothing. The value of these schools is not only that they are good, but that they are good for something. The ATS mission statement continues: "the improvement and enhancement of theological schools *for the benefit of communities of faith and the broader public*." A theological school is worth the investment because the learning, teaching, and research that comprise its work serve communities of faith and inform the mission of those communities in the world. Theological schools are worth their salt as faculty teach, research, and write in ways that prepare men and women, lay and ordained, for the various works of ministry, and as teachers, students, and graduates give voice to a religious message in an era where neither popular nor intellectual culture seems inclined to listen.

I chose the image of earthen vessels as a metaphor for theological schools for many reasons beyond the ones identified in the introduction. A vessel has instrumental value, not terminal value. Terminal values are good, in and of themselves. Love's goodness, for example, depends on what love is, not what love may do. Instrumental values are good to the extent that a proper function is served. Like a vessel, a theological school has instrumental value. It is good because it serves a function that enriches the life and leadership of communities of faith and their witness to a broader world. If a vessel cannot hold water, it is not very useful. If a vessel is so beautiful that it ceases to be used, it may add beauty to a room but it no longer serves the function for which it was designed. Theological schools are not good because they have great histories, or wonderful facilities, or distinguished faculties. They are good to the extent that they cultivate the learning, knowledge, skills, sensitivities, and perceptions that the church needs for its leaders.

What do schools need to do to ensure their future contribution? I have focused attention in this essay on the processes of theological schools — learning, teaching, research, governing, and administering. Along the way, I have described what these processes were designed to do and how they can be shaped to serve the future. A school is more than processes, of course; it is people. As I conclude, I want to turn attention to the people in theological schools: board members, donors, administrators, faculty, students, and ecclesial communities.

Board members are far more crucial to the integrity and capacity of theological schools in the present than they were in the past, and they will be even more important in the future. In fact, without thoughtful and creative board work, many schools may not have a future at all. This present moment — when so much is changing in the church, in the church's social location in the culture, in the patterns of financial support for theological schools, when so much seems to be up in the air — calls boards to careful and thoughtful work to secure needed resources, to require the careful management of resources that are presently available, and to engage the generative tasks necessary for schools to be positioned and poised for the future. The path that leads from the present to the future will require more hard decisions than easy ones, more imagination than repetition, and more creative commitment than casual consensus. Theological schools need governing boards that understand how integral these schools are to the vitality of communities of faith and how critical communities of faith are to a society that needs moral understanding translated into social witness, religious commitment translated into a winsome religious voice, and mercy translated into acts of service and care. Boards cannot bring theological schools into the future alone, but no school will make it without the careful work of boards that hold the mission and resources of the school in trust.

Individual contributors, and the family foundations that these contributors are forming, need to provide both the financial support for the present work of theological schools and the resources necessary for their future vitality. There was a time, not too long ago, when denominations provided the majority of funding necessary for seminaries to operate. The church that benefited most directly from the work of the schools paid much of their cost. For the most part, that is no longer the case. Many denominational budgets are strapped, resulting in decisions to curtail programs and mission efforts and reduce support for institutions that the church values but can no longer fund. The future for most theological schools will be financed by individual gifts for scholarships and operating costs, by gifts for the renewal and construction of facilities, and by gifts to endow the future of the school's work. Gifts to theological schools do not translate into the immediate and empirical outcomes that gifts to some charities make possible; they translate into long-term good done congregation by congregation, ministry setting by ministry setting. Theological schools need a generation of generous donors who will give willingly to fund the present and make the future possible.

Senior administrators need to provide careful management of current resources, clarity and consistency in the implementation of the school's mission, and a commitment to solve current problems in ways that pave the way to the future. None of these tasks is easy administrative work, and none is accomplished in a gentle eight-hour day. Administration has become dramatically more important to the vitality of schools across the past fifty years, a trend that will be even more evident in years to come. Senior administrative work will build the future of theological schools by intelligence, imagination, hard work, and faithfulness to the school's mission. Absent any of these, administrative leaders will not do what needs to be done. There was a time when seminary presidencies were platforms for leading the denomination that sponsored the school. That has changed. The platform in many denominations has changed from leaders of schools to the pastors of the largest and most influential congregations. Presidents increasingly need to focus on leadership of the school, finding and nurturing the school's constituency, discerning and implementing its mission, and finding and growing its resources. This is an era in which theological school leaders need to be motivated by commitment and calling, willing to work hard, and able to pull the best of the school's history into the future.

Faculty members are the primary resource for implementing the school's mission. For many students, the faculty *is* the school. They listen to what faculty have to say and are formed by how faculty construct intellectual resolutions to religious issues and problems. Faculty are crucial to the future of theological schools, but the future will require them to think carefully about the intellectual work that the church needs and the education their students need.

Theological faculty exercise both a prophetic and priestly role. The Hebrew prophets were called to speak moral truth to power, usually from outside the system, and more than once, they were punished by the power they addressed. Hebrew priests were a special class, and they exercised their religious leadership within the ecclesial and national structures of ancient Israel. They represented God to the people and the people to God. It was not always safe work. The high priest was to wear particular vestments and perform particular duties in the most holy place which, if not followed, were thought to lead to his death. Sometimes seminary faculty have an overdeveloped sense of their prophetic role and an underdeveloped perspective on their priestly role. Some are called to speak prophetically, but they do so from the protections of academic employment and are far less vulnerable than the Hebrew prophets. Most are called to a more priestly role in ecclesial systems, to do the work those systems need and to serve their constituencies. The future may be a time when the stress in communities of faith and in the practice of ministry calls for considerable priestly work, and faculty need to affirm its value. Faculty members perform a priestly role when they turn their intellectual and scholarly skills toward the issues that communities of faith need most. Faculty fulfill a priestly role by attending carefully to the changing situation in North American Christianity and North America's changing place in global Christianity.

Students are near the center of the work of theological schools. They are not the center — these schools have missions that are larger than educating students — but if there were no students, there would be no schools. Students enroll in ATS schools for many reasons. Some come in response to compelling calls to ministry while others are searching to see if they are called to vocational religious work. Still others enroll because they want to explore the dimensions of their faith. All of these motivations for undertaking a seminary education are legitimate. Whatever the reasons that brought them to seminary, students should leave school with the understanding that theological learning is not a possession for individual enjoyment but a stewardship on behalf of the communities that have lived the tradition and handed it on. All theological learning is practical. It leads to an understanding of the good that should be enacted, of truthfulness that should be affirmed, of tradition that should be remembered, of practices to avoid and practices to emulate, of understanding that pertains to responsible life of faith. Students embody much of the present work of the schools and most of the future of leadership in congregations, denominations, and the organizations that contribute to and extend their work.

The Future of Theological Schools

What is the future of graduate, professional education for ministry? Many have a dim view of what the future will or can be. Others are not sure but are more worried about demise than hopeful about success. Still others, though not sure, are more hopeful. There is almost no one who is unreservedly optimistic. I am more hopeful than worried and, every once in a while, unreservedly optimistic. The present seems to be a discontinuous point in history. Most often, the present flows with some degree of predictability from the past, in a continuous manner. Sometimes, however, the path from the present to the future is discontinuous. Nothing in the horse and buggy era could have predicted the social changes that the automobile would bring. If it is a discontinuous time, why am I hopeful and on many days even optimistic?

Schools are institutions, and institutions have an incredible capacity to endure. They can weather hardship for a very long time. Schools are not invincible, however, and institutions cannot be sustained without a mission that stakeholders value. Some schools will close, but they have done so in every era in the two-hundred-year history of North American theological schools. While some schools have closed during the past fifty years, accredited ATS membership has grown by almost one hundred schools. Every historical era includes the founding of new schools and the closing or merger of others. Someone at an ATS meeting several years ago quoted an unnamed expert on theological education as saying that as many as half of the current schools would close or merge in the next ten years. We are now halfway through the time frame of that statement, and the pace of closings has been very slow, so far — one school. Some schools are in the emergency room and a few are on artificial life support, but most are continuing, developing new institutional skills, and learning to be effective agents of theological education in changing and turbulent times.

I am hopeful because it is the nature and gift of institutions to find ways to change to meet what the future needs, whatever that turns out to be. Theological schools will change less than many are predicting and more than others want. People who want theological schools to return to the forms and patterns that they imagine them to have had fifty years ago will likely be disappointed, as will those who are convinced that schools in the future will bear little similarity to the ones we have now. Theological schools will continue to provide formational education, but with the increasing diversity of ministerial occupations, the nature of that formation will focus more on Christian identity than pastoral identity. Theological schools will continue to provide viable patterns of education with less money than this kind of education truly requires, and they will continue to cost more than their critics think they should. Theological schools will be more similar to other forms of higher education than some would like, and more distinct from higher education conventions than others would prefer. Theological schools will respond to changes in the church more slowly than the church would like and more quickly than academic purists think necessary. The future will be multidirectional, and schools will reflect more varied and variegated educational forms than they do now. I am convinced, however, that among these many changes, theological schools will have a recognizable presence in the future, that their educational capacity will be enhanced, and that they will be educating ministers and priests, laypersons working in parishes and congregations, and persons who long to learn in depth about the faith that gives them life.

What should schools concentrate on as they move into this discontinuous future with its multidirectional change? They should do what they do best, what they were designed to do: serve as centers of learning, teaching, and theological research.

Theological schools are good at learning and teaching, and they should get better at both. Persons will need to be educated for work in congregations, parishes, and the manifold contexts of religious work. Learning for ministry results in knowing texts, traditions, and practices of the community of faith, and knowing them deeply enough that learners are formed by what they know. Learning for ministry also cultivates the skills necessary to negotiate the complex ministerial tasks of working with people, exercising leadership, struggling through conflict, making sense of human ambiguity, and getting the job done faithfully. Theological schools need to teach with an educational imagination informed by the changing contours of congregational life and religious expression. This kind of teaching requires a deep sensitivity to the places where graduates will serve and appreciation for the work they will do. Learning and teaching in theological schools will continue to be oriented to theological understanding, an understanding that leads to responsible life in faith.

Theological schools are good at theological research, and they should increase this work. The congregational pace is hectic, and few pastors have time to generate the scholarship the church needs. Theological scholars need to be in libraries poring over the records of millennia past in search of guidance for the future. They also need to be busy in congregations, closely discerning new contexts for old questions and new answers from a dependable tradition. The church needs deep and substantive intellectual work. Theological schools are centers of intellectual energy and talent that should be expended on research agenda that inform the life, work, and witness of communities of faith.

As I listen to some church leaders and read some analyses of the needs of the church, the intellectual work of research or learning more than strategies for ministry seems to be in disrepute. It is perceived as a luxury that can no longer be afforded or a useless way to engage the practical difficulties that churches face. To some, intellectual work that does not have an immediate application feels like counting and color-sorting the deck chairs on the Titanic. Even a cursory glance at church history, however, refutes this assessment. The church was struggling to define what it was and what it believed when St. Paul wrote his letters. The church was struggling with new life in an ancient world when Augustine wrote the *City of God*. Paul's letters have practical advice, but it is often housed in complex theological affirmations that had never been made before. Augustine had a lot to do as the Bishop of Hippo, and in the middle of leading a young church, he wrote theological treatises that have informed the understanding of Christian believers to this day. I wonder if someone in his day complained that he didn't get done what needed to be done because he was writing that book. We live in a time in which useful and relevant information is crucial for congregational life and vitality, but Christian faith is not just about the problems of parishes and congregations at a given point in time. It is about an understanding of faithfulness and hope that emerges from thousands of years of study and research. Good intellectual work may be an important way in which the Spirit speaks afresh to guide this and future ages.

Another verse in that King James Bible my parents gave me that was especially difficult to understand was in John 3: "the wind bloweth where it listeth, and thou hearest the sound thereof, but canst not tell whence it cometh, and whither it goeth. . . ." I remember thinking that I should be able to understand this verse — after all, it was from the chapter I had been taught was central to the New Testament message — but I couldn't. I remember writing it out in longhand, dropping the "eths," but it remained a mystery. Fifty years later, I have discovered that my not understanding was, in some ways, an accurate understanding. God's presence, like the wind, does not reveal its origin or destination; its movement can be felt, and its effect experienced, but the ways of God are, from beginning to end, mysterious. The God of ages past is the God of ages to come. The wind will blow. The purposes of God will sustain communities of faith and call new ones into being. Those communities will need pastors and teachers who know the story, who have learned a theological wisdom pertaining to responsible life in faith, and who are capable of leading communities in pursuit of God's vision for the human family. These pastors and teachers will need schools because schools provide the kind of learning they most need. Schools are earthen vessels that serve this particular function exceedingly well. The Spirit of God moves, and we do not know "whence it cometh or whither it goeth," but we can be confident that God will be up to something, working out God's purposes, calling into being what those purposes require for any age.

Index